How to use E

C000070433

①
Find a time you
can read the
Bible each day

Issue 103

The 92 daily readings in this issue
of *Explore* are designed to help you
understand and apply the Bible as
you read it each day.

②
Find a place
where you
can be quiet
and think

It's serious!

We suggest that you allow 15 minutes each day to work
through the Bible passage with the notes. It should be a meal,
not a snack! Readings from other parts of the Bible can throw
valuable light on the study passage. These cross-references can be
skipped if you are already feeling full up, but will expand your grasp
of the Bible. *Explore* uses the NIV2011 Bible translation, but you can
also use it with the NIV1984 or ESV translations.

③
Ask God to help
you understand

Sometimes a prayer box will encourage you to stop and pray
through the lessons—but it is always important to allow time
to pray for God's Spirit to bring his word to life, and to shape
the way we think and live through it.

④
Carefully read
through the
Bible passage
for today

We're serious!

All of us who work on *Explore* share
a passion for getting the Bible into
people's lives. We fiercely hold to
the Bible as God's word—to
honour and follow, not
to explain away.

⑤
Study the
verses with
Explore, taking
time to think

⑥
Pray about
what you
have read

the good book
COMPANY

BIBLICAL | RELEVANT | ACCESSIBLE

Welcome

Tim Thornborough is the Publishing Director at The Good Book Company

Being a Christian isn't a skill you learn, like cooking or stone skipping. Nor is it a lifestyle choice, like the kind of clothes you wear, or the people you choose to hang out with. It's about having a real relationship with the living God through his Son, Jesus Christ. The Bible tells us that this relationship is like a marriage.

It's important to start with this, because many Christians view the practice of daily Bible-reading as a Christian duty, or a hard discipline that is just one more thing to get done in our busy modern lives.

But the Bible is God speaking to us: opening his mind to us on how he thinks, what he wants for us and what his plans are for the world. And most importantly, it tells us what he has done for us in sending his Son, Jesus Christ, into the world. It's the way the Spirit shows Jesus to us, and changes us as we gaze upon his glory.

The Bible is not a manual. It's a love letter. And as with any love letter, we'll want to treasure it, and make time to read and re-read it, so we know we are loved, and discover how we can please the one who loves us. Here are a few suggestions for making your daily time with God more of a joy than a burden:

◆ *Time:* Find a time when you will not be disturbed, and when the cobwebs are cleared from your mind. Many people have found that the morning is the best time as it sets you up for the day. If you're not a "morning person", then last thing at night or a mid-morning break might suit you better. Whatever works for you is right for you.

◆ *Place:* Jesus says that we are not to make a great show of our religion *(see Matthew 6:5-6)*, but rather, to pray with the door to our room shut. Some people plan to get to work a few minutes earlier and get their Bible out in an office, break room or some other quiet corner.

◆ *Prayer:* Although *Explore* helps with specific prayer ideas from the passage, you should try to develop your own lists to pray through. Use the flap inside the back cover to help with this. And allow what you read in the Scriptures to shape what you pray for yourself, for the world and for others.

◆ *Share:* As the saying goes: *expression deepens impression.* So try to cultivate the habit of sharing with others what you have learned. Why not join our Facebook group (links below) to share your encouragements, questions and prayer requests? Search for *Explore: For your daily walk with God.*

And remember, *it's quality, not quantity, that counts:* better to think briefly about a single verse than to skim through pages without absorbing anything, because it's about developing your relationship with the living God. The sign that your daily time with God is real is when you start to love him more and serve him more wholeheartedly.

GENESIS: Good to bad

We pick up the narrative in Genesis where we left off last time. The universe has been created, and God is resting. But now the tone, language and focus changes.

Read Genesis 2:4-7

❓ *We've already read about the creation of humanity in 1:26-28. So why do you think this second account is here?*

❓ *What are the differences? Can you explain them?*

Some people believe the account which begins in Genesis 2:4 is different from, contradictory with and even inferior to the account in 1:1 – 2:3. We can't agree if we respect Scripture as the word of God. Nevertheless, there are differences from chapter 1.

Genesis 1 could be described as an overture, while Genesis 2 is like individual musical "movements". Genesis 1 gives us the big picture—all the themes are there, caught up in one grand and flowing account. But a massive amount is left unsaid, so Genesis 2 begins to give us a closer look.

Waiting for Adam

❓ *What is said here about the plants?*

❓ *What is said about the water?*

❓ *How might you describe the earth before man's creation?*

Genesis 2 focuses on the human world (not the whole world, but that for which humankind would be responsible) and humankind's relationships with and within it. Creation is waiting for people to come along and the earth is unfruitful because there is "no one to work (literally "to serve")

the ground". As every gardener knows, you don't want rain when there is no one to mow the lawn! So there is water in this primitive earth (v 6), but it is not yet harnessed beneficially.

This is the situation in and for which the man is created. He is to serve the earth.

Significantly, therefore, he is formed "from the dust of the ground" (ground' = *adamah* in Hebrew, from which comes "Adam" i.e. "man"). Although man has humble origins, his life comes directly from God, who breathes "living breath" into him.

···· TIME OUT ····································

Read John 20:22

❓ *What is the significance of Jesus' action here?*

❓ *What would you say to someone who believes that we are "nothing but" chemicals and animal instincts?*

⌃ Pray

"Dust to dust, ashes to ashes…"

Remember who you are—fearfully and wonderfully made, and yet weak and frail—and praise your Creator.

For God's glory

Today's psalm is a profound reflection on facing crushing, numbing disaster. How does Asaph, the writer, deal with what seems to be God abandoning them to their enemies?

A desolate scene

Read Psalm 79:1-4

> ❷ *What do God's enemies see as they observe the situation in Judah?*

The psalm opens with scenes of devastation and desolation after foreign powers have attacked and destroyed Jerusalem. The piles of dead bodies mean that the temple itself is defiled. It is God's servants, his people, who have been slaughtered. The neighbouring nations look on with contempt and they mock. The implication is that God is mocked by this too (v 1-4).

A desperate cry

Read Psalm 79:5-13

> ❷ *What does Asaph think should motivate God to deliver his people?*

The plea goes up, "How long?" Is this permanent judgment? Has God turned against them for ever? Will he come to their rescue? Surely it should be the enemy who are punished because they do not know and do not worship God (v 4-7)?

The cause of judgment has been building up through a long history of stubborn rebellion (see Psalm 78) but Asaph begs that his generation are not judged for the sins of past generations. It's not that they are any more worthy of God's favour. However, his plea is that God will hear the cry of repentance from this generation. The plea is for

God to help, God to save—for forgiveness. *Why?* It is for God's own glory so that the nations cannot doubt his existence (Psalm 79:8-10a). The turning point he pleads for is that God will vindicate *himself* and defeat their enemies. Just as the nations have looked on and mocked God, now Israel will look on and praise God (v 10b-13).

Jerusalem would experience such desolation several times, including by the Babylonians in 581 BC. Christ himself would suffer the ultimate desolation of a brutal death at Calvary. His resurrection demonstrates God's vindication and victory.

⌄ Apply

Grace means that the gospel isn't all about you and me. God's very purpose in sending Jesus to die and rise is so that he will be glorified. This is not about narcissism. Rather, if God himself is the one of greatest worth and glory, it is right that he should receive all the honour and praise. This means that even our evangelism is an act of worship. As the Westminster Shorter Catechism says, our reason for living is *to glorify him and enjoy him for ever*.

⌃ Pray

Thank God for saving you. Pray that you will be given opportunities to speak about him today so that his name will be glorified.

Eden

The Garden of Eden is a powerful image for us to grapple with. It speaks of God's intentions for the world and for people. It speaks of a world of innocence and glory.

Read Genesis 2:8-14

❷ *What do you think was the difference between the world in general at this point and the Garden of Eden?*
❷ *What do we learn about God's provision for mankind?*
❷ *And God's purpose for mankind?*

Eden

The world was waiting to be filled and subdued. Note that at the beginning the world was not perfect (i.e. not complete). But a garden is (at least in intention) an ordered and cultivated place. So it was here that God caused attractive plants and fruitful trees to grow. These trees were not just "good for food" but "pleasing to the eye". God provides beauty as well as nourishment.

The Garden of Eden was designed to show what the world was intended to become under the care of humanity.

⌃ Pray

God is the first "artist" as well as being an architect and builder. He has created beauty as well as practicality. Think of a time and place when you have been stunned by the beauty he has made. Give praise to our awesome God for his creative brilliance.

The two trees

❷ *Look at verse 9. What was unique about Eden?*
❷ *Look ahead at verses 15-17. For what other purpose was Eden created?*

Uniquely, two special trees grew at the centre of this garden—"the tree of life" and "the tree of the knowledge of good and evil". Eden was more than a pleasant location or a model of what man would achieve—it was a testing ground, where man's obedience to God would be tested and where issues of eternity would be decided.

❷ *Can you spot the parallel between the gardens of Eden and Gethsemane?*

Gethsemane was also a testing ground—where one man's obedience to God was tested to the farthest limits, and again, where issues of eternal life were decided.

Beyond Eden

Verses 10-14 give us an idea of the landscape and features of God's world beyond Eden. The picture of abundant water and the details about mineral resources conjure up an image of a land ripe for exploration and enjoyment. At this stage, the future seems bright! God's good world awaits its human rulers.

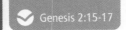
Good and evil

Most people today would say that personal fulfilment is impossible without complete autonomy—freedom from being ruled by someone else. Genesis 2 says different.

Provision

Read Genesis 2:15-17

> ❷ *Look back at 1:26-28. What are the limits of our "rule" and our "likeness" to God?*
> ❷ *Does life in the garden look or feel like slavery or servitude? If not, what?*

The man was put not only in a place prepared by God (Eden) but also in a relationship with God—under his rule. But a rule, wonderfully, like no other. Notice God's two commands: *Eat anything you like... but not that.* Adam had abundant blessing from God but not moral autonomy. In Eden, Adam found God's blessing under God's rule. Eden is actually a picture of the kingdom of God—blessing under God's rule is the present privilege and future destiny of Christians today.

Purpose

> ❷ *If you were able to go back and ask Adam what he thought of his job, what do you imagine his reply might be?*

God's blessing included purpose and meaning. Adam was to "work" or "keep" the garden (like a park-keeper in charge of a park). Our purpose is found in showing God's likeness by ruling the creation under us.

Prohibition

> ❷ *What do you think is meant by "the knowledge of good and evil" (2:17)?*

This term appears in Deuteronomy 1:39 (little children "do not yet know good from bad") and in 1 Kings 3:9 (kings need to "distinguish between right and wrong").

But Adam wasn't a child—he surely knew there is "good and evil". He had a capacity and (like kings) a *responsibility* to make right judgments, otherwise God could not have tested him. So here "the knowledge of good and evil" must mean something else. God's prohibition was intended to show that Adam must not presume to decide between right and wrong independently of God. To do so would mean death (v 17), for it would be to separate from God, and actually oppose him.

⌄ Apply

> ❷ *People say, "You can't tell me what to do". Why are they passionate about this?*

Although we are outside Eden, like Adam, we too must not presume to tell God what is right or wrong.

Read Romans 12:2

Pray for obedience to what God's word says is right and wrong.

On my own

In this perfect garden, there yet remains something that is not quite right. This outwardly simple narrative has surprising depths to it.

All alone

Read Genesis 2:18-20

> ❓ *What suddenly surprising statement appears in these verses (compare 1:4, 10, 12, 18, 21, 25, 31)?*
> ❓ *Who makes this statement?*

Seven times in Genesis 1 we read that God's creation is *good*. Now, for the first time, something is "not good"—specifically, it is "not good for the man to be alone". Adam isn't complaining of loneliness. It is God, not Adam, who announces what is "not good". There is a lack of completeness—something more is needed before mankind is finished and God can declare everything "very good" (1:31).

The missing link

> ❓ *What is needed?*
> ❓ *What for, do you think?*

God also defines what is missing—Adam needs "a helper". Elsewhere in Scripture, this refers to the help God provides in a crisis (Psalm 121:2) or help given by an ally in war (2 Kings 14:26). What Adam needs is not help with the housework but strengthening from someone "suitable for him".

▼ Apply

> ❓ *Is being independent a strength or potential weakness, do you think?*

Remember, God designed us for togetherness.

The X Factor

A sort of talent parade follows (Genesis 2:19).

> ❓ *What does Adam do here?*
> ❓ *How is he achieving the purpose for which he's been made (see yesterday's notes)?*
> ❓ *How does this demonstrate that there is "no suitable helper" (compare 1:28)?*

Animals have "strengths" that humans lack. Think of what elephants, horses or dogs can do that we can't. Yet none of these is the "suitable helper"—they can't supply the strengthening that Adam specifically needs.

Notice that God waits to see how Adam will name each creature. He gives Adam autonomy here because, by naming the animals, Adam is ruling them, as he was designed to. But the helper is to be with Adam in this (Genesis 1:28—God spoke to "them").

▲ Pray

Thank God that he has not made us to be alone. Pray for those who strengthen you, and for people you know who are lonely.

> ❓ *How will you strengthen others today?*

The woman

Adam needs strengthening to be complete, but with what kind of strength? It's not physical strengthening, and it's not just company—it can't come from another man.

Read Genesis 2:21-25

❓ *Why do you think some modern minds find verse 22 offensive?*

❓ *What do the woman's origins tell us about her identity (v 23)?*

❓ *How does Adam greet the woman, and what does it tell us about her and him?*

Just a spare rib?

Is woman simply man's "spare rib"? That's how many today view the message of verse 22. But look at the welcome the man gives to the woman in verse 23. She is one with him, even though she is separate from him. She is of his very essence—bone of his bone and flesh of his flesh—and yet she is not a man.

❓ *What outcome did God intend from his creation of the woman (v 24)?*

Verse 24 tells us that "that is why" (the same-but-different nature of the woman) people separate from their parents and unite in marriage. And in the rest of the Bible, sexual union is seen as recreating the one-flesh ideal of Adam and Eve, even when that union is itself far from ideal (see, for example, 1 Corinthians 6:16).

☑ Apply

Sex is good: God made it! Christians above all should regard sex and sexuality as a wonderful and beautiful thing. It is a vital and beautiful way that God enables the very first commandment in the Bible ("be fruitful and increase in number", Genesis 1:28).

United with Christ

But marriage is not the ultimate goal for humanity. In the New Testament the one- flesh union of marriage is a picture of the greater "one spirit" union of each believer with Christ (1 Corinthians 6:17). The creation of Eve points us to our ultimate dignity and the destination of redeemed humanity—union with Christ.

At this stage, nakedness and sexuality bring no shame (Genesis 2:25). Far from it! They are the very creation of God himself—the one who makes all things "good".

⌃ Pray

Many see human marriage as the solution to our "aloneness", but the true solution is divine marriage (Revelation 19:9).

Pray for those (perhaps yourself) who feel loneliness and long for marriage—to be strengthened by God himself.

And pray for the marriages of people you know, that there would be a mutual strengthening, love and unity as God intended.

The snake

Revelation 12:9 confirms something that most of us assume but which is not actually explicit in today's reading.

Read Genesis 3:1-5

Crafty questions

- ❓ *How does the snake's question exaggerate God's prohibition? (Compare 3:1 with 2:16-17.)*
- ❓ *What idea about God would this begin to create in Eve's mind?*
- ❓ *How does the woman's answer (3:2-3) exaggerate God's prohibition?*

"You must not touch it" (3:3) is an addition to God's words in 2:17. Had God said more to Adam than we read in chapter 2? Had Adam tried to put his own "fence" around God's law in what he said to Eve? Or did Eve make this up herself? We do not know.

Whatever the answer, Eve has been drawn into a damaging dialogue with the enemy about God's will and his truth. Every time he speaks, the devil sows doubts and denials of God's words and character and truth into Eve's mind.

⌄ Apply

"Your enemy the devil prowls around like a roaring lion" (1 Peter 5:8). Dialogue is usually the best approach to resolving moral issues. But sometimes it is better just to run for your life!

- ❓ *What situations do you think you would need to run from?*

Deadly denials

- ❓ *What is the devil trying to suggest about God in Genesis 3:4-5?*

The snake moves from subtle suggestion to outright denial, "You will not certainly die" (v 4)—implying that God has lied. And from there it is only a small step to trashing God's motives, "God knows ... you will be like God" (v 5)—suggesting God wants to keep the best for himself, so he's not generous at all but selfish.

So far, humans have accepted God's limit on their moral autonomy—they know of good and evil, but have not "taken the fruit". They have accepted that God defines what is good and evil, and have trusted what he has communicated through his word. But now they are offered the opportunity, no longer to trust but to see for themselves (v 5).

The pattern of lies and subtle appeals to our selfish desires continue today as the key part of Satan's devices. He tells us that things are ours by right, that we will mature, and be properly grown up, that the truth will be revealed to us, if only we will...

⌃ Pray

How is your trust in God's character and word? Pray for God's help in resisting the devil's crafty tactics.

Heading for a fall

It's sometimes hard to read a passage like this because of the wealth of cultural ideas that have been loaded onto it. It is the worst day in history...

A delicious prospect

Read Genesis 3:6-7

❓ *Find three reasons why eating the forbidden fruit must have seemed like a good idea.*

❓ *An essential component of sin is the suppression of the truth (Romans 1:18). What truth must Eve have suppressed to take this step?*

Eve fell into sin for a series of compelling reasons—the fruit of the tree appeared nourishing, attractive and could make you brainy (Genesis 3:6)! But her overwhelming desire for these things led her to "forget" that God had forbidden it, and accept the enemy's slander of her Creator, who had shown her nothing other than lavish generosity and total love.

A devastating outcome

❓ *Where was Adam all the time that Eve was being tempted?*

❓ *Look at what happened immediately after they ate the fruit. How did this both deliver and depart from what had been promised (v 5)?*

Not surprisingly, Eve gave some to her husband. She wanted him to have what she had got, and he was willing to take it, in spite of knowing what God had said. This story has been used in church history to represent women as the tempters, and responsible for the fall. In fact, Adam appears to have been beside her during the whole conversation. His inaction to correct her thinking, challenge the snake, deny the lies about God, and to defend God's honour, are equally, if not more culpable.

They were promised that the fruit would help them see clearly (v 5). And it did, but what they saw first were themselves in a new and unpleasant light. Whereas before their nakedness left them unashamed (2:25), now they felt shame and tried to cover up.

Shame is a complex emotion. In some societies it drives people to suicide. Recollections of shame last far longer than other memories, even though it is often caused by small things. We feel shame intensely because it connects with the depths of our being. Shame is also about the views of others—we are ashamed before them. Adam and Eve hid, not from God initially, but simply from view. Their attempts to cover themselves with leaves, however, were as pathetic as they are understandable.

⌃ Pray

Are there things that you feel ashamed of? Christ bore our shame as well as our sin on the cross (see Hebrews 12:2).

There is no need to hide away from him. Show him your gratitude, right now...

Restore us, O Lord

How can we keep going in a world full of so much fear, suffering and sorrow? As we saw in the previous psalms, Asaph is no stranger to pain, disaster and doubt...

A diet of tears

Read Psalm 80

- ❓ *What imagery is used to describe God?*
- ❓ *How are God's people described?*
- ❓ *What is the repeated refrain through the psalm?*

The psalm opens with a plea for God to listen. We see his sovereign greatness and his loving kindness together. He is exalted above the cherubim, but draws close as the Shepherd of his people (v 1-2). Once again, the plea is "How long?" The people are derided and mocked. It is as though they are feeding on their own tears and suffering (v 4-6).

Israel is compared to a vine, transplanted from Egypt to Canaan by God. He drove out their enemies like a gardener clearing the ground of rocks and weeds. He expected it to be fruitful (v 9-11). Instead, the vine has been cut down and trampled. How can this have happened? The psalmist recognises that God's intervention is needed. The plea of repentance comes with a promise to turn back to God and trust him (v 12-18).

Much of this psalm is a lament. A lot of worship songs focus on praise and joy but there is a place for lament where we recognise the sorrow and suffering that sin causes. However, lament is turned into hope by the refrain that punctuates the psalm. That refrain is a plea that God will restore us. Asaph prays that God will lift up our heads so we can see God's face again (v 3, 7, 19).

⌄ Apply

When Jesus meets Bartimaeus in Jericho (Mark 10:46-52), he asks him, "What do you want me to do for you?" The blind beggar responds, "I want to see". As Jesus healed his eyes, the first thing Bartimaeus would have seen is the face of his Saviour. Our greatest need is to see Jesus for who he is: his beauty, his glory, his majesty. We are promised that one day we will see him face to face (1 John 3:1-2). In the meantime, as we are reminded of the gospel, our gaze is lifted up from the sometimes fearful and distressing circumstances we find ourselves in and we learn to cling on to Christ.

⌃ Pray

Tell God about the specific things that cause you distress. Punctuate your prayer with the refrain: "Restore us, God Almighty; make your face shine on us, that we may be saved".

Blame-storming

The man and woman hide, filled with shame. And then they hear a rustling in the undergrowth. How will they react?

Read Genesis 3:8-13

God could be heard going about the garden (v 8). Could this be God's Son before his incarnation? It's not entirely clear—the Hebrew could mean God's voice, and does not require that he was walking on foot. Yet clearly, this familiar sound meant Adam and Eve knew it was time to hide.

Respect

❷ *Why do you think God asked: "Where are you?" (v 9)?*

❷ *Adam's answer (v 10) isn't the whole truth. What's the real reason for his fear?*

God isn't ignorant of Adam's whereabouts. Rather, he shows Adam respect by calling the man to come to him willingly. But the intimate relationship between them has been broken. Where there was once openness, there is now fear. Adam and Eve haven't only tried to cover themselves from view—they have tried to hide themselves from God. What's more, the cover-up is more than physical. Adam doesn't say: "I was afraid because I had disobeyed" but "because I was naked".

❷ *Why do you think God asked: "Who told you?" (v 11)?*

God already knows mankind has disobeyed—that's why they now see themselves shamefully and fear him.

Their nakedness was not a problem under God's rule until an outsider changed that perspective. God's question invites them to confess and repent.

Blame

What comes instead is blame. Adam manages to blame simultaneously his wife and God—"the woman you put here with me" (v 12). Eve is slightly more honest: "The snake deceived me, and I ate" (v 13).

❷ *How has God's order and purpose for man, woman and animals been overturned?*

Man was made to rule the animals, yet he has listened to them. Eve was made to strengthen Adam, yet she has weakened him. Adam was told to obey God, yet he has followed his wife into sin.

☑ Apply

Don't blame others for your own disobedience to God. When you are tempted, God also provides a way out (1 Corinthians 10:13).

Confess any disobedience to God and ask for the strength and courage to obey him in the future. And ask the Lord for reliable helpers around you to strengthen you against the devil's devious lies.

The curse

God blessed his creation three times (see Genesis 1:22, 28; 2:3). Now we read of the opposite as God curses his creation, beginning with the serpent.

The snake

Read Genesis 3:14

❓ *How is the serpent's position in the animal kingdom affected by God's curse (see also v 1)?*

Whereas the serpent was once renowned for his superiority above the other animals, now he will be cursed "above" them, which means being reduced "below" them—crawling on his belly, where he will literally "eat dust". People often want to know if snakes originally had legs! Biologists believe they did but Genesis draws a veil over this.

The promise

Read Genesis 3:15

❓ *The serpent successfully deceived Eve, but in what way is this a hollow success?*

Astonishingly, we move from curse to promise! It's true that the serpent deceived Eve by his cunning (see 2 Corinthians 11:3). But he didn't win *possession* of Eve. Instead, there is to be warfare between him and the woman, and in future generations. The mention of offspring does not mean Satan gives birth to future demons, but that the conflict is to be ongoing—not confined to Eden.

The outcome of the conflict will be the destruction of the serpent—though at substantial cost to his destroyer. The Hebrew for the level of damage is the same for both, but the object of the damage is significantly different: *he will crush/strike your head; you will strike/crush his heel.*

Verse 15 is known as the "first gospel" because it would, of course, be fulfilled by Jesus. And through him, all Christians share that same victory...

☑ Apply

"They overcame [the devil] by the blood of the Lamb and by the word of their testimony; they did not love their lives so much as to shrink from death" (Revelation 12:11).

Satan is a defeated enemy, but not yet a dead enemy. Therefore we must be "alert and of sober mind" (1 Peter 5:8).

Pray for faithfulness and effectiveness in the conflict with Satan and sin.

The pain

Just as there was a "chain of blame" moving down from the man, via the woman, to the serpent, so now there is a chain of curse moving in the other direction.

Motherhood miseries

Read Genesis 3:16

❓ *What two areas of a woman's life are affected by God's curse?*

❓ *Does this feel unfair to you? Why?*

The serpent has been told that Eve's offspring would eventually defeat him. Now, however, Eve hears that producing offspring will be no easy matter. It will be characterised by severe pain—the word translated "pains" (NIV) can mean struggle or sorrow. So the miseries that were to accompany motherhood were not only physical ones (see Luke 2:35).

⌃ Pray

Pray for pregnant women who you know, that God might keep them safe. And for mothers who are in sorrow over difficult or wayward children.

❓ *How might you help them today?*

Husband hassles

❓ *What do you think "your desire will be for your husband" means (compare Genesis 4:7)?*

The wording of 3:16b exactly parallels the warning about sin given to Cain in 4:7, where God warns Cain that sin will control him if he doesn't struggle against it. If the example of sin and Cain is anything to go by, Eve's desire for her husband would not be sexual but a struggle for control.

This certainly makes sense in the context— Eve had earlier sought to do what was "best" in her eyes for Adam, even though she should have known it was wrong. Perhaps this temptation to "improve" her man would be built into their relationship as a permanent reminder of what went wrong.

⌃ Pray

Pray for understanding in your relationships with members of the opposite sex.

And pray for the redeemed marriages within your congregation, that they would resist the pull of these temptations and show the beautiful (and evangelistic!) qualities of marriage as it was meant to be...

The dust

Finally, God turns to Adam and puts his finger on his sin. The analysis of his wrongs, and what flows from them are truly devastating.

Adam's sin

Read Genesis 3:17-19

> ❷ *What specifically was Adam's sin?*
> ❷ *What is the curse he must bear?*

The NIV says: "Because you listened to your wife..." Elsewhere, however, the full phrase "listened to the voice of" means "obeyed" (see, for example, 22:18; 27:13). It's not that a man should never listen to a woman, but that Adam should not have done what Eve said when it went against what God had said. It is no excuse to say, "I was only obeying orders..."

The cursed ground

> ❷ *Why did God curse the ground (see 2:15)?*

Eve was cursed in her specialist realm of childbearing, and Adam in his specialist realm of ground-keeping. Throughout the Old Testament, this idea of the cursed ground or land recurs (see Deuteronomy 24:4b; 29:27; Jeremiah 44:22).

Mankind depends on the land as well as ruling it, and the specific result of this curse is that food production now becomes a problem. The word for "painful toil" is the same as that used for "painful labour" in Genesis 3:16. Instead of freely available fruit to eat (2:16), the ground now produces thorns and thistles, and only after sweaty toil will there be any edible produce (3:19).

⌄ Apply

Don't overvalue work. By its very nature it is "sweaty toil" that leads to frustration, as well as meaningful activity.

Cursed into the ground

> ❷ *Why did God curse Adam to return to the ground (compare 2:17)?*
> ❷ *Why was this appropriate (compare 2:7)?*

God warned Adam that disobeying his command would bring death (2:17)—it wouldn't be instantaneous but it would be absolutely certain. Adam was formed from the ground—his very name means "earth". Taken from humble beginnings, he now faces a humiliating end. The words "dust to dust, ashes to ashes" may sound dignified at a funeral service, but they really express a shocking fact. We are made to image God, but through sin, we become nothing but floor sweepings.

⌃ Pray

Read 1 Corinthians 15:47, 49

Praise God for his great salvation, which raises us from the dust of death to a glorious hope of a secure future with Christ.

Life goes on

The Anglican funeral service reminds us that "in the midst of life we are in death"—but it's also true that, under God, in the midst of death we can experience life.

Continuation
Read Genesis 3:20-24

❓ *What sign of hope can be found in Adam's choice of name for his wife?*

❓ *And what greater hope will this lead to (see 3:15 and Galatians 4:4)?*

Eve is to be "the mother of all the living" (Genesis 3:20). Life will go on—a remarkable affirmation of hope amid the curses and tears of Genesis 3. What's more, the one who will bring eternal life has already been promised—and will be "born of a woman" (Galatians 4:4).

Covering

❓ *How does God's covering for Adam and Eve compare with theirs (Genesis 3:7)?*

❓ *What does God's covering cost?*

God himself now shows the way ahead by providing animal skins for the man and the woman. Clearly, their own attempts at covering themselves up were a pathetic failure. Now they have an effective covering—but at a cost, for these garments are the skins of dead animals (v 21). Atonement—a word whose root itself means "covering"—will only ever come with the taking of life.

Cut off

❓ *What's the purpose of the cherubim and flaming sword (v 24)?*

By eating the forbidden fruit, Adam and Eve have become "like God"—they have decided what's good and evil—challenging God's right to decide and separating themselves from him. They mustn't become immortal like God as well. This means separation from the source of life in the garden.

The cherubim and the flaming sword make it clear that there's no way back. In the future, the tree of life will be found somewhere else entirely—in Christ, who, "'himself bore our sins' in his body on the cross, so that we might die to sins and live for righteousness" (1 Peter 2:24).

▲ Pray

Fallen nature constantly reminds us that life depends on the death of others.

Read Hebrews 9:22

Thank God that the outcome of Genesis 1 – 3 is not death and dust but the cross and glory.

Creation and fall

Today we'll take the opportunity to review the first three chapters of Genesis and think in more depth about what we have seen.

What exactly are we reading in these first three chapters of Genesis? Some would reject them as mythological creation stories—similar to (and as silly as) the many stories circulating in the ancient world about how the world came to be. But anyone who has read any of those, will instantly realise that what we have here is far more profound, powerful and poignant than, for example, stories about how humans came from the armpits of an ice giant (Norse); that we are made out of corn (Mayan); or that creation came into being when a giant god called Bumba fell ill and puked us all into existence (the Bushongo people of Congo).

God and our world

Read Genesis 1

- ❷ *How is God portrayed in Genesis 1?*
- ❷ *What is his relationship to creation?*
- ❷ *How do you think this fits, or doesn't fit, with scientific views on the origins of the universe?*

Genesis 1 is absolutely foundational to our thinking about who God is and why we are here. He crafts creation—and humanity— carefully, lovingly and intentionally; he delights over it. He is not absent from the world, but intimately involved with it. And it is purposeful, not accidental. The universe has meaning, and we have meaning and value, because we are created by God in his image.

⌄ Apply

- ❷ *Why are these principles so important as a foundation for our understanding of:*
  - *human value and dignity?*
  - *the care of creation?*
  - *our approach to life as a whole?*

The fall

- ❷ *How does the narrative of the fall in Genesis 2 and 3 shape our understanding of human nature now?*
- ❷ *Why is it so important to hold together the two key observations of these chapters—that the world is made good, but that it is also fallen?*

Salvation

- ❷ *What signs are there in these three chapters that this is not the end of the story—that God has a plan for undoing the effects of the fall?*

⌄ Apply

- ❷ *How would you respond to someone who says that Christians follow an irrelevant ancient myth?*

Joyful obedience

Do you ever struggle to "get going" when worship songs are sung at church? It's easy to feel cold and distant while others around seem joyful and praise-filled...

Kick starter

Read Psalm 81

❓ *What are God's people called to do?*
❓ *What is the basis for God's command?*
❓ *How do they respond?*

Psalm 81 begins with an invitation to sing and worship. The worship is to be rich, accompanied by all kinds of musical instruments, and was intended to mark the great festivals of ancient Israel. Mouths were to be filled with song (v 1-3).

The call to worship God is more than an invitation. It is a command. Specifically, it is the festival that has been commanded (v 4-5). The command is rooted in God's saving acts when he delivered the people from slavery in Egypt. True obedience arises out of grace (v 6-7). The call to true worship is exclusive; God's people are not to be distracted by other gods (v 8-9). Furthermore, worship arises out of God's provision. God says, "Open wide your mouth and I will fill it" (v 10). In the context of rescue, feasting and provision, this may point to God feeding his people. However, it is also about the God who, through his saving acts, gives us the words to say. He fills our mouths with song.

Sadly, as the psalmists often lament, the response of God's people has not been trust and obedience. Instead, they hardened their hearts against him. They rebelled (v 11-12).

They did not listen. God responds as much in sorrow as in anger. There is a pleading. If only the people would trust him and return to him, they could enjoy his protection and provision (v 13-16).

⌄ Apply

Sometimes we can think of the call to obey God as conflicting with grace and love. The risk is that we see God as like a strict teacher or policeman. In the wisdom literature (Psalms, Proverbs, Job etc.), we see instead that God is portrayed as a good shepherd and a good Father. It is in the context of his love and goodness to us that he invites us to obey him. It's a call to trust him and depend upon him with gratitude. This is not an austere obligation, but rather an invitation to joyful obedience.

⌃ Pray

What have you got to be thankful for when you think of God's specific provision and protection for you?

How can you express that thankfulness in joyful obedience?

Commit to God the specific areas of your life where you need to trust and obey today.

1 TIMOTHY: The secret

Who wrote this letter, and to whom? Why did he write—what is it all about? The first question is answered in the opening verses—the second question later in the letter.

Who?

Read 1 Timothy 1:1-2

The letter opens, as was common, by describing the sender and the recipient.

> ❷ Who wrote it, and how does he describe himself (v 1)?
> ❷ Who received it, and how does the writer describe their relationship (v 2)?
> ❷ How should this affect how we read the letter, do you think?

An apostle was somebody who was sent on a mission—something like an ambassador. This was by divine appointment, not self-selection—read 2:7. But if Timothy is Paul's "son in the faith" (1:2), why does Paul need to underline that he (Paul) is, truthfully, a God-appointed apostle? The best explanation is that this letter was not a private correspondence but intended to be a public letter of recommendation for Timothy—something like us giving a reference for someone to a potential new employer.

Why?

Read 1 Timothy 3:14-16

> ❷ In Paul's physical absence, what will this letter enable Timothy to know (v 14-15)?
> ❷ What will spring from knowing the "mystery" of which Paul speaks in v 16?

Paul is writing to this man of God to tell him how to conduct himself among the people of God. It is not about how he may *like* to conduct himself, but how he *must* conduct himself among God's household.

3:16 is the most important verse in the letter, but it causes many a reader to scratch their head. "Mystery" is a key word for Paul, but it is not a helpful translation because it does not really mean "mystery"! Paul is not speaking of something impossible to understand, or deeply spiritual, or irrational. Paul means "secret": something that was once hidden and has now been made public. For example, I may choose to hide my birthday from you. So it becomes a secret, unless and until I reveal it to you.

As we relate to the one true God and Father of our Lord Jesus Christ, we pursue right behaviour—but that is not what "godliness" is. "Godliness" is about relating to your God rightly. The great secret of godliness is found not in our approach to God but in his approach to us. It is not in our moral or religious activities, but in God's gospel of his Son, who appeared in the flesh, was vindicated by the Spirit, seen by angels, preached among the nations, believed on in the world and taken up in glory.

⌃ Pray

Pray that, as you read this letter, you would come to more fully understand and appreciate how God has come to you in Jesus, and that this would shape the way you live in response to that.

Truth matters

Our world is in love with love. And sometimes our message of love melds easily with the world's love. Yet, to our world, Paul's charge in 1:3 sounds anything but loving...

Read 1 Timothy 1:3-7

❷ *What does Paul want Timothy to command particular people (v 3-4a)?*

❷ *What is the goal in commanding these people to stop (v 5)?*

But... where's the love in Paul telling Timothy to impose his view and what he thinks on another, in opposition to their view and what they think? Surely we have moved beyond somebody charging others to be silent.

❷ *But why is it so important that Timothy commands these people to stop teaching (v 4, 6-7)?*

These false teachers have swerved from the foundational motivation of Paul and Timothy—from the gospel. And, having deviated from this, they have turned towards vain, empty and meaningless discussions. Theirs was not an immediate denial of the gospel but a departure from its spiritual effects that led on to the emptiness of falsehood. The result is ignorant and arrogant teachers, who want to be teachers of the law but do not know what they are talking about (v 7).

···· TIME OUT ···

❷ *Have you witnessed or experienced teachers like this within the church?*

❷ *What damaging effects did they have on the gospel faith of others?*

❷ *How popular were they?*

The central problem with this false teaching is that it does not promote the "stewardship" (v 4, ESV) from God. The stewardship of God is God's plan of salvation—his plan and management. The whole programme of God is not about speculative myths and genealogies—it is not an intellectual game to be played. God's programme is about salvation by faith and restored relationship with himself. God's plan is fulfilled in a man who said he was *"the* way and *the* truth and *the* life"* (John 14:6, emphasis added).

Truth is found and taught not simply in affirmations but also in rebuttals. When errors are opposed, it highlights both the details and the importance of the truth. Yet to oppose errors and those who teach them requires not only a firm grasp of the truth but also the emotional strength to keep standing firm. Charging false teachers to desist from their teaching is not consistent with this world's version of love, but it does flow necessarily from Christ's love for his church.

⌃ Pray

Thank God for the truth he has revealed in his Son, the Lord Jesus. Thank God for his flawless word, all about his Son. Thank God for those who teach you his gospel from his word, and equip you to spot and counter error, rather than falling for it. Pray that they would continue to have the conviction and emotional energy to stand courageously.

Law, gospel and us

Understanding the role of the Old Testament law in Christian life has been an abiding problem. The gospel brings liberty, but we struggle not to live in legalism or licence.

Read 1 Timothy 1:8-11

Paul's instruction to Timothy here is not the sum total of what he says about the law, but it is a very important part of the New Testament teaching about God's law.

The law in 1 Timothy

- ❷ *What does Paul affirm (v 8)? What condition ("if...") does he attach?*
- ❷ *Who is the law "for" (v 9-11)? What do you understand Paul to mean by this?*
- ❷ *What does Paul say about the gospel (v 11)?*

The law in the OT

God gave the law to Israel with great fanfare at Mount Sinai. While the people of Israel were willing to enter into covenant with God, they didn't really want to hear what he had to say. Their fearful and rebellious hearts kept them from embracing God's law—and their subsequent history demonstrated a remarkable resistance to it. The promise of the new covenant is not so much of a new law, but rather a new heart that is able to receive the law—**read Jeremiah 31:31-34**.

So who is the law for?

People who are "righteous" (1 Timothy 1:9) do not need the law to condemn them or constrain them. They do what is right. So,

Paul says, the law is given for people who are not right—in particular the "lawbreakers", who live out their lawlessness in immorality.

So do Christians, justified by God's grace, now still need the Old Testament law? Yes—first, because through our Lord Jesus Christ, this is the law that is written on our hearts by the Spirit, who moves us to obey it as we hear it. And second, because while we live in this world, our sinful desires of lawlessness keep waging war with the Spirit.

Notice that Paul says that the lawless deeds of verses 9-10 are contrary to the sound doctrine that conforms to the gospel (v 11). The things the law opposes are the very things the gospel also opposes. The very reason the law had to be given is not ignored by the gospel, but rather addressed in the gospel. To set the law against the gospel is a great mistake. The law drives us to the gospel, and the gospel moves us to obey the law.

⌄ Apply

- ❷ *Are you more tempted to live in legalism (obeying God's law to earn/keep his favour) or in licence (disobeying God's law because you are right with him by grace)? In what ways?*
- ❷ *How does Paul's teaching about the law here help you to obey it out of a gospel motivation? What will change in your behaviour as you do this?*

He came to save you

Have you ever considered how surprising, and kind, it is that God has not only saved you through faith in his Son but also gives you work to do in proclaiming his Son?

Paul had. He never grew less than awe-struck about it.

Grace for a blasphemer
Read 1 Timothy 1:12-14

❓ *What is Paul grateful for (v 12)?*
❓ *Why is this particularly amazing (v 13)?*

To modern ears, blasphemy is not such a great crime. But in God's world, blasphemy is so serious as to be the one unforgivable sin (Mark 3:28-30). We have reduced "blasphemy" to swearing—vulgar, meaningless references to God. But Paul's blasphemy was much more than that. His was the intentional opposition to Jesus seen in his murderous persecution of Christians. He set out to destroy Jesus' messianic claim by persecuting his followers.

What does it mean that Paul received mercy "because I acted in ignorance and unbelief" (1 Timothy 1:13)? Does that mean ignorant unbelief is excusable? In the Law of Moses, God differentiates between sins that are unintentional and those which express defiance—sinning "with a high hand"(e.g. Numbers 15:27-31, ESV). Saul of Tarsus was forgiven his blasphemy because it was the unintentional sin of ignorance and unbelief. He needed salvation in the same way that a lost sheep, straying by its own stupidity, culpable yet helpless, needs rescue. He didn't intend to blaspheme the Lord—just the reverse: he thought he was honouring him.

A trustworthy saying
Read 1 Timothy 1:15-17

❓ *How is Jesus' work described (v 15)?*
❓ *How does Paul define himself (v 15)?*
❓ *How would this view of himself enable him to more fully appreciate all that Jesus came to do for sinners?*

Notice what Paul says Christ displayed in saving him. He could have rightly said "mercy", "kindness" or "power"—but he writes "immense patience" (v 16). God is immensely patient. He is slow to anger, and in his slowness he endures the ongoing sinfulness of people. He could have rightly finished the world the day Adam ate the fruit. He could have killed Saul when he zealously took part in killing Christ's servant Stephen (Acts 7:58; 8:1). But he had other plans for the world, and for Saul. Christ's "immense patience" with Paul gives hope to all who are still alive—there is still time to believe in him for eternal life.

❓ *What does Paul's view of himself and of Christ move him to do (1 Timothy 1:17)?*

Pray

Consider your own sinfulness, and the truth that "Christ Jesus came into the world to save sinners"—even Paul, and even you.

Then use verses 12 and 17 to praise and thank your Saviour.

First of all…

Paul is entrusting his gospel ministry to Timothy. This passage shows us that the stakes could not be higher—and points to where Timothy should begin with this weighty charge.

High stakes

Read 1 Timothy 1:18-20

- ❷ *What is "this command" (v 18—look back to v 3-4)?*
- ❷ *Why does it matter so much that Timothy does this (v 19-20)?*

Paul's aim in handing these men over to Satan is that they may learn not to blaspheme. Paul had been a blasphemer—though he acted in ignorance and unbelief (v 13). This pair are apparently becoming blasphemers in knowledge and defiance. They are therefore in greater danger of going beyond forgiveness (Mark 3:28-30).

Our first recourse

Read 1 Timothy 2:1-4

- ❷ *What does Paul urge Timothy to do "first of all" (v 1)?*

It is not clear how this command relates to the problem of false teaching and wandering from the faith that Timothy is to address. But we should not miss the simple point: when faced with any challenge or command, our first recourse should be to prayer.

⌄ Apply

- ❷ *What are you in the habit of praying about, and why?*

What to pray for

- ❷ *What must Timothy pray for (v 1-2)?*
- ❷ *Why (v 2)?*

God appoints governments as his servants for our good (Romans 13:1-7). The decisions of these powerful people can facilitate or frustrate the ability of others to lead the kind of life that pleases God (1 Timothy 2:3). So we are to pray for those in high position, that they might enable us to live a good life that pleases God. Our rulers' decisions about work hours, weekends, justice, marriage laws, censorship or any other matter affect the way we live, making it easier or harder to live a God-pleasing life (a life based on the secret of godliness, 3:14-16).

- ❷ *What does God desire (2:3-4)?*
- ❷ *So if we are blessed with the ability to "live peaceful and quiet lives", how would God like us to use them, do you think?*

⌄ Apply

- ❷ *How much freedom do your "rulers" (your government, your boss at work, and so on) allow you to worship Christ in how you live, and proclaim Christ in how you speak?*
- ❷ *How are you going to use your freedom to do these things?*

Finish this study on prayer by spending time praying…

One God, one mediator

If Christians are free to live godly lives, then God is pleased—because living in godliness means speaking the gospel, and proclaiming the truth is how people are saved.

What God wants

Read 1 Timothy 2:3-4

Like a lifeguard or lifesaver at the pool or the beach, God desires to save whoever needs saving.

> ❷ *What do people need to know in order to be saved (v 4)?*

The great truth

Read 1 Timothy 2:5-7

> ❷ *What is "the truth" that people need to know to be saved (v 5-6)?*
> ❷ *How does this truth mean that the gospel is both completely inclusive and totally exclusive?*

This is the great statement of monotheism: "For [or "because"] there is one God" (v 5). The logic of there being only one God is that there is only one God for all of humanity to worship and serve. And there is also only one God who can save us; and he has done so by coming in the person of Jesus to become our mediator. A mediator is someone who brings about reconciliation between two parties who are otherwise in disagreement or at war. That mediator will need to enjoy the confidence of both parties to persuade them to settle their accounts and make peace. Humans may want any number of mediators, but the only one acceptable to God is his Son. He became human ("the man Christ Jesus") in order to be able to represent God to us and us to God.

We are the offending party, and God is the one offended against. The method of Christ's mediatory work is spelled out in verse 6: he "gave himself as a ransom for all". Jesus himself described his sacrificial death as giving a ransom (Matthew 20:28; Mark 10:45), on behalf of and as a substitute for others. This ransoming death of Jesus is the testimony—the witness to and argument for—the character of God the Saviour, who desires all people to be saved.

The gospel of Jesus is not offered to a single nation or a particular people group. It is the announcement that the one God over all humanity does not desire the death of any sinner, but that each would turn and live (Ezekiel 18:23, 32)—and that in Christ's mediatory, ransoming death any and every man and woman, whatever their position in society or on earth, may be saved.

> ❷ *What is Paul's role in the great plan of "God our Saviour" (1 Timothy 2:7)?*

✔ Apply

We are not called to be apostles, but we are called to be heralds.

> ❷ *God wants all people to be saved. Do you want all people around you to be saved?*
> ❷ *What are you doing to tell them of the one God and one mediator?*

Mortality

Despite what naysayers suggest, religion remains hugely popular—if not formal religion, then a collection of vague superstitions. What does the Bible think of these "gods"?

Useless

Read Psalm 82

- ❓ *What plea have the gods failed to heed?*
- ❓ *What becomes of the gods?*
- ❓ *How does Asaph ask God to respond?*

Asaph pictures a heavenly court with Yahweh gathering together the gods, or heavenly beings. These beings seem to have authority and power over regions of the world, but they are not using it for good. Instead, they bring oppression. This is not left unanswered. God brings judgment (v 1-2).

First of all, God sets out the reason for judgment. The gods have failed to hear the plea for justice and mercy to be given to the vulnerable and needy. The gods should have been acting to protect the poor, widows and orphans, but instead have exploited them for their own gain (v 3-4). The reason for this is that they are ignorant of God's goodness and his ways; they are like those who stumble around in the dark (v 5). So, God's judgment is that they will lose their immortality; becoming like humans, they will taste death (v 6-7).

We cannot depend on the powers and authorities that rule over this world for justice. So, we turn with Asaph at the end of the psalm and look to the Lord alone to bring this about (v 8).

TIME OUT

Who are the "gods" that Asaph refers to? We are not meant to think of them as divine rivals to God; they are created beings. The Old Testament sometimes uses the word *Elohim* to refer to spiritual beings such as angels and demons. The psalm does seem to suggest that these have some influence in human affairs. However, it is likely that we are meant to read the psalm as a figurative representation, with "the gods" standing in for earthly powers and rulers. At the same time, we should remember that there is a demonic power behind idolatrous systems (see 1 Corinthians 10:20).

⌄ Apply

God's judgment here should challenge us. Do we value and prioritise what God values? Do we seek justice and mercy where we are? What would it mean for you and your church to show concern for the needs of "the poor and the oppressed" in your community?

⌃ Pray

Identify a specific example of injustice that you are aware of. Pray for those who are suffering that they might know relief.

Pray that God will bring the oppressor to repentance.

Men and women

These verses speak into a controversy that has divided Christian thinking for a generation. We should be wary of our own natural bias towards one direction or another.

A word to men

Read 1 Timothy 2:8

- ❓ *What does Paul want men to do?*
- ❓ *What must they avoid as they do this?*
- ❓ *Why might men need to be told both the positive and the negative here, do you think?*

The key is not the physical posture of hand-lifting. In the Bible many different and mutually exclusive postures of prayer are described. The essential posture is that of the contrite and humble heart, and a peaceful outlook. Anger and fighting are, in most senses, the opposite of prayer.

A word to women

Read 1 Timothy 2:9-15

- ❓ *What is your instinctive reaction to these verses? Why?*

Paul raises two issues: apparel and learning.

- ❓ *What does he say about women's clothes?*

Paul is calling upon women to think for themselves about how they adorn themselves so that they can present themselves in a way that is consistent with their Christian faith. His examples of immodest dressing are just illustrations. We must not become legalistic, as if women must never braid their hair or wear a gold ring or a pearl necklace.

- ❓ *What does he say about how women learn from the Scriptures (v 11-12)?*

"Quiet" can refer to silence, but equally it can refer to a quiet demeanour (see 1 Peter 3:4). That appears to be the sense here.

- ❓ *What two reasons does Paul give for his commands here (1 Timothy 2:13-14)?*

God's order of creation (v 13) is significant in the Bible's understanding of authority. God gave the role of leadership to Adam. Men and women are equal, but they are not the same. And in the fall, God judged the man for following his wife's leading rather than stepping up to lead himself (Genesis 3:17). Eve was deceived, but Adam was not deceived—he had directly received God's command (2:16-17). He wilfully, knowingly became a sinner.

1 Timothy 2:15 is confusing (and space is short!): suffice it to say that it is *not* saying that every woman must have children, nor that every woman who has children is saved, but that the work of the gospel restores the order of creation.

⌄ Apply

- ❓ *What will it look like for you, as a man or a woman, to live out these verses faithfully and wisely?*
- ❓ *Are there aspects of these verses that you need to pray or think about or discuss more fully? How will you do so?*

A noble thing

Next, Paul sets out the qualifications for taking on something "noble". But what is this noble thing, and who should undertake it?

What the task is

Read 1 Timothy 3:1-7

❓ *What aspiration does Paul have in mind (v 1)?*

❓ *What difference does it make that Paul says this is a noble task rather than "role", "job" or "office", do you think?*

Each denomination has their particular pattern of ministry and ministers, and each uses this passage to give titles and names to their leaders. So different denominations use the same name to refer to ministries that are different in their appointment, responsibilities and activities (e.g. bishops, priests, and deacons, or elders and teaching elders, or pastors and deacons). It helps to note that the thing Paul says is noble to aspire to is not a position but a task.

❓ *What is the task (end of v 5)?*

To "manage"and "take care of" has the sense of being in charge and caring for. This is indeed a noble task, for the church is a "pillar and foundation of the truth" (v 15).

The qualities required

The character of the men who give leadership in God's household is critically important to the health of the church. In a sense, Paul's list of qualities in v 2-5 should be growing in all Christian men. Nearly all are about character rather than competencies.

❓ *For each, what would this quality look like in daily life in your particular culture and church?*

❓ *What limitations does Paul add (v 6-7)?*

First, worldly leadership is about significance, importance and power. Christian leadership is about service and sacrificial love. A recent convert may not yet see the difference and, imbued with worldly thinking, fall prey to pride. Second, if an overseer has given outsiders no reason to think well of him, or (worse) every reason to think poorly of him, he may well fall into such disgrace that he has been trapped by the devil and is brought down.

⌄ Apply

❓ *Men: to what extent are these characteristics descriptive of you? Where can you be encouraged? How do you need to change?*

❓ *Women: to what extent are these characteristics the ones you most admire in men? (Of course, many of them are equally to be pursued by women.)*

⌃ Pray

Pray for the overseers in your church: that these characteristics would more and more describe them, that God would protect them from serious failure in these areas, and that they would manage your church faithfully.

In the same way…

From one noble task, Paul turns to another—that of the deacon. But again, we have to ask: What is a deacon, and who should undertake this task?

What is a deacon?

Among the problems of translating this word into modern English as "deacon" is the different meaning that various ecclesiastical traditions give to the word.

Read 1 Timothy 4:6

The word translated as "servant" (ESV) or (less helpfully!) "minister" (NIV) here is translated "deacon" in 3:8.

> ❷ *What difference does that make to our understanding of what a deacon might be?*

It would be better in verses 8-13 to translate the word in the usual way as "servant" and work out from the passage what Paul was talking about.

In this sense, then, these verses speak to all of us, for all of us are called to be servants of the greatest of all Servants. We are never more like Jesus than when we serve others well (Mark 10:42-45; Philippians 2:5-11).

What is a deacon like?

Read 1 Timothy 3:8-13

> ❷ *What are the similarities between the character required to be an overseer (v 1-7) and a deacon here?*
> ❷ *What are the differences?*

Verse 11 could be referring to women who are deacons/servants (as the NIV suggests) or to the wives of men who are deacons/servants (as the ESV renders it). The Greek is unclear, but the point is: whether we think of servants' wives or female servants, their character and behaviour is to be the same as that of the male "servants".

Any attempt to be precise about the work of the servants is still as doomed to failure as any precise description of the work of the overseer. Timothy is being told how one ought to behave in the household of God. The keys to that behaviour are what we would call morality and ethics, not performance and task. Being a deacon or overseer are activities to be sought and prized, rather than offices to be pursued or wielded. The person who has the characteristics described here for deacons will be someone who serves humbly, wisely and helpfully in God's household.

☑ Apply

Think about your attitude towards, commitment to and activity within your own local church.

> ❷ *Would other church members describe you as a "servant"? Why/why not?*

As you did in yesterday's study, check through this list of characteristics.

> ❷ *Which do you need to grow in? About which can you give thanks that the Spirit has already been growing you in?*

Godliness and gratitude

A modern guide to godliness might be called "The Six Steps of Godliness" and contain a list of things to do. But Paul gives a list of six things God has already done in Jesus.

Godliness revealed
Read 1 Timothy 3:14-16

3:14-16 is the centre-point of 1 Timothy, and it is the centre of Paul's argument and gives the reason for him writing. It reveals the "mystery" (or better "secret") of godliness—what God has done for us. So, godliness requires no rules to keep, no steps to follow, no habits to form, no activities to engage in, no clubs to join and no fees to pay, and there are no key performance indicators to achieve. Godliness is not about us but about God. (The NIV translation of v 16a is unhelpful; the ESV translates it far better, simply as "Great indeed, we confess, is the mystery of godliness...")

> ❷ *What six things has God done in Jesus (v 16)?*

The first of these is usually understood to refer to the incarnation, when God became flesh. But it is much more likely to refer to Jesus' bodily resurrection, when he appeared (was manifested) repeatedly to the disciples.

In the first century, and for a Jewish man like Paul, the idea that the Jewish Messiah would be "believed on in the world" was wonderful and slightly extraordinary. But that is what Paul was seeing all around him—as the gospel went out to the nations, all manner of people were coming to faith in Jesus.

> ❷ *What will knowing the "mystery of godliness" (the gospel) allow Timothy, and all Christians, to know (v 15)?*
> ❸ *What goes wrong when professing Christians get these two—believing the gospel and conducting yourself rightly—the other way round to how Paul does?*

Gratitude for creation
Read 1 Timothy 4:1-5

> ❷ *What problem does Paul introduce in verses 1-2?*

This is a harsh description, but it is mild compared to the damage these people do to others (2 Timothy 2:17-18).

> ❷ *What are these false teachers saying (1 Timothy 4:3)?*
> ❷ *What is the error in this (v 4-5)?*

Ascetics say the world is evil; materialists say this is accidental—neither worldview sees it as good, nor do they give humans spiritual responsibility for it. The Bible does.

☑ Apply

> ❷ *How do verses 4-5 show us how to enjoy good things in this creation without worshipping them?*
> ❷ *How can you make sure that you are receiving "with thanksgiving" the good things that God has given you?*

Hard training

The truth matters, and it is eternally wonderful. And so false teaching matters, and it is infinitely damaging. Therefore Timothy's ministry is going to be hard work…

Point it out

Read 1 Timothy 4:6-10

❓ *What are the "things" Timothy must point out to the church (v 1-5)?*

Timothy is not to remain silent about error and falsehood but to expose error by teaching the truth: "the truths of the faith and of the good teaching that you have followed" (v 6).

Labour and strive

❓ *What is Timothy not to do, and what is he to do (v 7)?*

❓ *What is the main point Paul wants to make in verse 8, do you think? (Hint: it is not about the benefits of physical exercise!)*

The metaphor here carries with it the sense of hard, persistent and repetitive work. Those who depart from the faith are "devoting themselves" to deceitful spirits and teachings of demons (v 1, ESV), just as the false teachers "devote themselves" to myths and endless genealogies in 1:4. Now Timothy is directed to train himself in accordance with or relation to godliness. This is not a command to practise Christian behaviour, but to commit himself to the gospel and its teaching, in contrast to pagan and silly myths. Training in this message is beneficial in ways that surpass the benefits of physical training.

There is not universal agreement as to whether the "trustworthy saying" mentioned in 4:9 is referring to the whole or parts of the preceding verse 8 or the following verse 10. Both sayings point to the salvation that is in Christ Jesus by the gospel message—the great confession of the secret of godliness.

The word "believe" (v 10) does not refer to an intellectual understanding (though that is part of it) but to trust. Trusting God, particularly trusting Jesus, God's only Son, and his death for us is the only way to receive salvation. Hope in the living God, who is the Saviour of all people, is an expression of such trust. So this verse is not teaching that all are saved.

❓ *What do the truths of verses 8 and 9 prompt Paul to do with his life (v 10)?*

The word "labour" is one of hard, wearying work; "strive" is a word meaning fighting and struggling.

❓ *What is this showing Timothy (and us) about Christian ministry?*

☑ Apply

❓ *Are you willing to listen to your church leader when they decide to point out falsehood in order to safeguard truth?*

❓ *Pastoring the household of God requires labouring and striving. How can you encourage your church's leaders today to keep going in their work?*

A diligent young pastor

Timothy's ministry is to have all the confidence of somebody who knows and teaches the truth of the gospel.

Commanded
Read 1 Timothy 4:11-12

❓ *What is Timothy to do with "these things"—all that Paul has told Timothy about discipleship so far (v 11)?*

Within the church Timothy is to *command* behaviour that befits the household of God.

☑ Apply

❓ *Are you willing to hear a command from the pulpit, based on God's word, to behave in a particular way?*

Problems with youth

In commanding anybody to do anything, there are times when we meet resistance.

❓ *What might be a particular reason for resistance to Timothy (v 12)?*
❓ *What is he to do about it (v 12)?*

In the Bible, the older tends to lead the younger. The idea of the younger leading or having any authority over the older is so rare as to be noticed as being unnatural (e.g. Genesis 25:23; John 1:15; Romans 9:12).

Paul's point in 1 Timothy 4:12 is that Timothy can't stop someone thinking negatively about him, but he can remove any reason for it— and he can even provide, in speech and conduct, reason for them to think of him positively.

Encouragement
Read 1 Timothy 4:13-16

❓ *What else does Paul tell him to do?*
  • *v 13*   • *v 14*   • *v 15*   • *v 16a*
❓ *What is the motivation for persevering in all this (v 16b)?*

The word "public" in "public reading" is not in the Greek of verse 13—it is assumed from two words that follow: "preaching" ("exhortation", ESV) and "teaching". **Read Acts 13:15 and 15:31.** Both times, the word of exhortation involves teaching people the meaning of the Bible. So Paul is telling Timothy to bring the encouragement of the Scriptures to the people, reading about and then teaching them of the great secret of godliness.

In 1 Timothy 4:14 Paul is taking Timothy back to the clear prophecy concerning the gift that God had given him, in order to encourage him to keep going, undaunted by opponents or those who look down on him.

☑ Apply

❓ *If you are in gospel ministry of some kind, how do these verses encourage you?*
❓ *If you are a church member who listens to the teaching of a younger person, are you in any danger of looking down on them in some way? How can you listen to and think of them in a way that helps you grow, and encourages them?*

When heaven is silent

It's a common accusation in the face of suffering, disaster, defeat. "Where was God when that happened?" But it's not just unbelievers who ask that question.

Read Psalm 83

> ❓ *What is Asaph disturbed about (v 1)?*
> ❓ *Who are the enemy really opposing?*
> ❓ *What are the enemy's apparent strengths?*
> ❓ *Where does the writer look back on to encourage himself?*
> ❓ *What does Asaph ask God to do to the enemy?*

Enemies are plotting against God's people. At first sight, it may seem that God himself is silent in the face of this oppression, but the psalmist prays that he will act because these enemies are not simply seeking to attack Israel. They are God's enemies: an attack on his people is an attack on God himself (v 1-2).

As well as believing that God himself is silent and distant, it is possible to become overwhelmed by the apparent strength and skill of the enemy. Asaph recognises that Israel's enemies are skilled and cunning (v 3, 5); they are united in purpose and Israel's very existence is at stake (v 4-8).

Yet Asaph is not overwhelmed. Instead, he turns to God for deliverance. He reminds God of the way he protected his people during the time of the judges, defeating nations that attacked them (v 9-12). He asks that as these enemies have sought the destruction of God's people, so they may experience a similar fate, experiencing shame and being brought to nothing (v 13-18).

TIME OUT

Imprecatory psalms are those that call upon God to bring judgment and destruction upon his people's enemies. If we struggle and are uncomfortable with the language of these songs, it is helpful to remember three things. First, that the cry arises out of severe suffering and oppression at the hands of evil by the psalmist and God's people. Second, that the enemy here is opposing God himself. And third, that the New Testament moves our focus from human enemies to spiritual ones.

⌄ Apply

Read Ephesians 6:10-17

> ❓ *Who or what is the enemy today?*
> ❓ *What weapons and defences do we have?*

We face a serious enemy. Satan seeks to tempt God's people to lead us into sin. His aim is to deceive and destroy. Just as Asaph and Israel had to trust God to defeat physical enemies, so too we must depend upon the Holy Spirit, the gospel and faith as we face spiritual attack. We can trust God to win the victory in our lives.

⌃ Pray

Where in your own life are you most keenly experiencing spiritual attack? Ask God to help you to resist temptation and to put to death sinful desires.

Bible in a year: Psalms 51 – 53 • Acts 20:17-38

Family values

We are not to treat those in our church as customers, nor even as citizens or neighbours. We are to relate to them as relatives—members of the same loving family.

Older and younger
Read 1 Timothy 5:1-2

❷ *Which relationships within the church does Paul have in view here?*

❷ *Imagine Timothy did the opposite of what Paul commands here. What problems would this cause?*

When it comes to older men and women, Paul is effectively saying, *As you would/ should honour your father and mother, so speak words of encouragement to these older saints.* When it comes to younger men and women, Timothy needs to treat them as equals, and not look down on them.

When it comes to his relationships with women younger than him, there is a difference that Timothy must remember—sexual drive (which is itself a good, created thing, but of course is so often used sinfully). Sinful men have a particular need for warning to behave "with absolute purity".

✔ Apply

Compare the way you think of, pray for and speak to older men and women, and younger people (especially those of the opposite sex) with the way Paul sets out here.

❷ *Is there anything you need to repent of (and perhaps seek forgiveness for)?*

❷ *How can you positively contribute to the strengthening of the family that your church is?*

Caring for widows
Read 1 Timothy 5:3-16

Paul now turns to an often-vulnerable group within the church: widows. He has in mind four different "kinds" of widows:

- Older widows without supportive family (v 4)
- Older God-fearing widows who have no relatives to support them (v 3, 5, 9-10)
- Older self-indulgent widows (v 6)
- Younger widows (v 11-15)

He also has different people in mind in terms of taking responsibility for widows: family (v 4, 8, 16), church (v 3, 16), and some widows themselves (v 13-14).

❷ *What is the best way to treat the widows in each group? Who bears responsibility for each group?*

Not all widows are the same—but Paul's concern is always the same: that Christians honour widows appropriately, and that Christian widows serve Christ appropriately.

✔ Apply

❷ *Do verses 3-16 apply to you personally in any way? If so, how?*

❷ *Do you need to speak to a pastor or trusted Christian friend to talk through how you are being called to live, or to support someone else in your family or church?*

Elders and workers

Now Paul turns to how a church is to treat its "elders", and how Christians are to honour God in their work relationships.

Worthy of honour
Read 1 Timothy 5:17-25

❓ *How does verse 17 help us see what an elder's ministry is?*

❓ *What kind of elders is Paul speaking of (v 17)?*

❓ *What are they worthy of (v 17)? What do verses 18-21 suggest this involves?*

This is not an invitation to sit in judgment over our elders. We are to obey and submit to our leaders, for they are answerable to God and not to us (Hebrews 13:17). Such answerability to God does not excuse their responsibility to manage well—it heightens it. The worthiness of an elder is attached not to his position but to his quality of managing. And Paul says that those elders who toil at preaching and teaching the word are managing well and therefore worthy of double honour.

The "double" is usually taken to refer to both senses of the word "honour" or "value", i.e. honour and honorarium. More likely, though, the next few verses spell out the two honours due to such men. They are to be paid (1 Timothy 5:18) and protected (v 19). In terms of protection, Paul knows leaders are always prone to being attacked. Their prominence makes them easy targets, and the easiest way to attack a message is to shoot the messengers. It is not as if leaders never fail, but the minimum standards of evidence must be strictly adhered to if justice is to be done.

❓ *How is Timothy to proceed if an accusation against an elder is:*
- *made?*   • *proved?*

The command to "reprove" in front of everyone indicates this is not about private sin.

❓ *Why is verse 21 so hard to obey when an accusation is made within the church?*

The warning against prejudging is paralleled with the command in verse 22: "Do not be hasty in the laying on of hands". The context of the passage may be that of "appointing" elders or showing acceptance of repentant sinners (or both)—either (or both) is to be done thoughtfully and carefully.

Worthy of respect
Read 1 Timothy 6:1-2a

❓ *How should slaves treat masters? Why?*

This is not the place to go into the Bible's teaching on slavery. But these verses remind us that God calls us to fulfil our obligations.

❓ *What principles do you see here that apply to your own life?*

⌃ Pray

Thank God for those who lead your church. Ask God to lead your church wisely in paying and protecting them well, and ask God to equip your leaders to teach you truth and exemplify the behaviour that flows from knowing Christ.

Contentment or disaster

Paul has already taken aim at the "austerity gospel" (4:1-5). Now, he sets his sights on the "prosperity gospel". They are opposite, but equally tragic and deadly, dangers.

Means to an end
Read 1 Timothy 6:2b-5

❓ *How does Paul describe those who "[do] not agree to the sound instruction of our Lord Jesus Christ" (v 3) in verse 4?*

"Godliness" (v 3, ESV) is all about what God has done for us in Christ Jesus. The false alternatives are all about what we have to do to be found acceptable to God. To be a teacher of such falsehoods requires somebody to have arrived (in their own estimation) at a superior position of perfection or enlightenment. There is always conceit involved in refusing to listen to Jesus.

❓ *What does the teaching of these false teachers result in (v 4b-5)?*
❓ *In what sense do they view being "godly" as a means to another end (v 5)?*

The key to contentment
Read 1 Timothy 6:6-10

❓ *What is truly a "great gain" (v 6)?*
❓ *How do v 7-8 show what Paul means by this type of attitude towards life?*

Paul is not saying that owning more than that is wrong in any moral sense (see verses 17-19). But he is saying that the possessions of this world are only for this world. The key lies in contentment: in being content with reality. With contentment, we can abound or be brought low, face plenty or hunger and abundance or need, and give in to neither grasping nor bitterness (Philippians 4:12).

❓ *What does the alternative to this kind of contentment lead to (1 Timothy 6:9)?*

Wanting to be rich is a fairly dormant desire for those of us who have no realistic possibility of ever gaining great wealth. Yet the massive amount of money spent on gambling, or the obsession with wealthy celebrities indicates how easily our dormant desire can awaken into godless activity.

The emphasis of v 10 is "root". This is the explanation of v 9—how the desire to be rich leads to disaster. The love of money is not the full flower of our sin but a starting point upon which all of it grows and is fed.

⌃ Pray

It is very hard to discern our own hearts when it comes to contentment, possessions and wealth (or the desire for it). Ask God to show you your heart as it really is, so that you can grow in the "great gain" of "godliness with contentment".

⌄ Apply

❓ *Do you believe verse 10? How does this reveal itself in your own attitude to money?*
❓ *Is verse 8 true of you? How does this reveal itself in your attitudes to good things that you don't have?*

Pursuing and keeping

"Man of God" is an Old Testament term used of the leader of God's people. In the New Testament, it is used only by Paul to speak to Timothy.

And this man of God must do two things...

A God-given effort
Read 1 Timothy 6:9-12

> ❷ *What is "all this" from which Timothy must "flee" (v 11)?*
> ❷ *What does this require him to do, positively (v 11)?*

This is a short list—not by any means a comprehensive list—of the desires and aspirations to be pursued not only by Timothy but also by anyone who would be a faithful servant of God. We cannot achieve any of them solely by our efforts of pursuit—they are all the gifts of God. Yet we should pursue each of them, not the least by continual prayer for God to develop them in us and us in them.

> ❷ *What else must Timothy do (v 12)?*

This is a metaphor for the effort someone has to put in when teaching and living the truth.

ᐱ Pray

No one grows as a Christian by accident. It requires our efforts and God's work (including his work in us to cause us to make that effort.)

> ❷ *Which of the desires and aspirations in verse 11 do you most need to "pursue"?*

Pray today, and each day, that God will equip you to make every effort to grow in this quality.

A command to keep
Read 1 Timothy 6:13-14

As in 5:21, the charge in 6:13 adds nothing to the logic of what Paul is saying, but raises the importance and significance of it. But what "this command" in verse 14 is, precisely, is unclear! Timothy is to flee evil and pursue righteousness, and he is to fight the good fight and take hold of eternal life. It could be all or any of these!

A reason to praise
Read 1 Timothy 6:15-16

Mention of the appearing of Jesus provokes an outpouring of praise to God. It is to this one and only God, who will display his Son again in his appearing, to whom Paul ascribes "honour and might for ever" (v 16). Who else would we want to rule us eternally?!

ᐱ Pray

Spend time praising this God, who has made himself known through the gospel of his Son, and then recommit yourself to living a life of obedience to his commands and faithfulness in his cause.

Giving and guarding

Now Paul concludes his letter to Timothy with a final word for the rich and a final exhortation to his "true son in the faith" (1:2).

Give

Read 1 Timothy 6:17-19

- ❓ *What are rich Christians not to be?*
- ❓ *What are they to do (v 17-18)?*
- ❓ *What motivation for living like this does verse 19 offer?*

Here is the consistent temptation for people of wealth, especially in a materialistic meritocracy—to think of ourselves as important, above the rest, high and significant. It is the temptation of the self-made to worship their maker! Added to this arrogance is the blindness of assuming that wealth gives security for the future (v 17). But "wealth ... is so uncertain". At any time, the economy can be devalued or our particular wealth can be destroyed. We know that—but we tend to ignore it.

All of us—and especially if we have any wealth—need to learn that it is more blessed to give than to receive (v 18; see Acts 20:35). Like the former thief who is to no longer take but to work in order to give (Ephesians 4:28), the rich are to do good with their wealth. They are to be like God—generous. By sharing in this way the wealth that God has provided, the rich will be rightly using money for eternity. For though money is the currency of this world (1 Timothy 6:7), it can be used for eternity (v 19). True life is not to be found in wealth but in knowing Jesus and using our wealth in his service.

☑ Apply

- ❓ *If someone else had a sight of your bank statement, would they think these verses should be a challenge to you, or an encouragement to you, or both? Why?*
- ❓ *In what sense do you need to hear the "command" here? What will change?*

Guard

Read 1 Timothy 6:20-21

- ❓ *What is Timothy to do, and what is he to take care not to do (v 20)?*

Timothy has been entrusted with a great responsibility (1:18), and the whole letter instructs him in how he is to behave. His task has been to silence opponents by laying the truth of how to behave in the household of faith before the church. Guarding what has been entrusted to him requires avoiding the empty nonsense of false knowledge. This matters—for gospel faith leads to life, and following false teaching means departing from that faith (6:21).

☐ Pray

Is there anyone you know who is swerving from the faith? Pray for them now, asking God to restore them to the gospel; and pray for yourself, that you might have opportunity to exhort them to return to faith in Christ, and him alone.

True godliness

As we finish our time in Paul's first letter to his "true son in the faith", Timothy, we're going to enjoy looking back over the letter as a whole.

So that you will know
Read 1 Timothy 3:14-16

- ❷ *Why was Paul writing to Timothy (v 14-15)?*
- ❷ *What great gospel truths are the foundation for the Christian life (v 16)?*
- ❷ *What "springs" from knowing the revealed "mystery" of God coming to us in Christ (v 16)?*

Prayer
Read 1 Timothy 2:1-8

- ❷ *What does a prayer life that springs from true godliness look like?*

Ministry
Read 1 Timothy 1:3-5; 4:6-16; 6:11-12

- ❷ *What does a ministry that springs from true godliness look like?*

Wealth and possessions
Read 1 Timothy 4:2-5; 6:6-10, 17-19

- ❷ *What does an attitude to good things in this world that springs from true godliness look like?*

Character
Read 1 Timothy 3:2-13

- ❷ *What does a character that springs from true godliness look like?*

⌄ Apply

- ❷ *What has most encouraged you in your time studying this letter?*
- ❷ *How has the Spirit been prompting you to change? Have you begun prayerfully to pursue that change?*
- ❷ *What one verse or passage would be useful for you to memorise?*

⌃ Pray

Use your answers to the Apply questions above to praise "God, the blessed and only Ruler, the King of kings and Lord of lords, who alone is immortal and who lives in unapproachable light" (6:15-16).

Home now

I had the privilege of reading this psalm with my mum by her hospital bed. She knew and believed these words, and she knew she was going home to be with Jesus.

Read Psalm 84

- ❓ *What is the psalmist yearning for?*
- ❓ *Why is one day in God's courts better than thousands elsewhere?*

The psalmists speak of their longing to be in God's house. They are describing the temple in Jerusalem. Unlike pagan temples, this was not a home for idols, as though God physically lived there, yet it was the place that represented God's presence with his people (v 1-2).

Their longing was not just to visit a building as tourists or even for a religious ceremony. They link being in God's house with being home. There's a sense of being wanderers away from the temple and away from home. In words later echoed by Jesus (Matthew 8:20), the psalmist points out that even the birds are provided with somewhere to shelter and rest (Psalm 84:3-4).

The longing for home and rest was expressed in pilgrimage. Each year, God's people would make their way to Jerusalem for one of the festivals. The pilgrimage would be a hard journey and involve passing through difficult terrain. The sons of Korah mention a specific valley and suggest it is a place of struggle, hardship and pain as they make their way home (v 5-7), but God strengthens them on the journey and provides abundant, refreshing water in a parched land (v 6).

And so the psalmist cries out to God. His heart's desire is to be as close to God's manifest presence as possible. So precious is time in God's presence that time with him equates to a thousand days elsewhere (v 8-12).

☑ Apply

The psalm gives us comfort, hope and assurance. We have a home with the Lord to look forward to. Jesus has gone to prepare a place for us and will come back for us. However, dwelling in God's presence is not just a future hope. When you put your trust in Jesus, God the Holy Spirit dwells in you. We do not have to make do with "one day in your courts": we can know God's constant presence with us now and in the future for we will live with him for ever in eternity.

⌃ Pray

Pray for those who are grieving and for those struggling with this life that they will find comfort, security and rest in Christ.

And pray that you would know this yearning for home as you walk in the world today.

GENESIS: Downfall

The story so far… The human race has been expelled from the Garden of Eden, losing any right to live as God's people, in his place, under his rule, enjoying his blessing.

Now we find out what life is like outside the garden and outside of the relationship with God we were created for.

Read Genesis 4:1

> ❷ *Compare 2:17. How does 4:1 help us to fine-tune our understanding of what God's judgment involves for us?*
> ❷ *After Eden, how does Eve feel about God, do you think?*

This verse shows how Eve begins to fulfil her name (like "living" in Hebrew, see 3:20) with the birth of Cain. But more significantly, it shows Adam and Eve have not lost all hope, nor have they entirely lost their relationship with God.

God is still involved…

The name Cain sounds like the Hebrew for "got". Eve says, "I have gotten a man with the help of the LORD" (ESV). The point is that Adam and Eve still see God, despite his judgment, as being actively involved in their lives, and Cain's birth as positive confirmation of this. God warned Adam that disobedience to his word would lead to death (2:17), yet now it is clear that life will go on. Death will come, but not yet.

… but man is still fallen

Today, the birth of a child is often celebrated as an antidote to old age and death. But it's not that simple. Adam and Eve's "innocent bundle of joy" would grow up to be the first murderer.

⌄ Apply

Even Hitler was cute once. Parents never have to teach their children disobedience—it comes naturally. Not just sickness and death, but sin entered the world through Adam (Romans 5:12). And every baby has that built-in, deadly flaw.

⌃ Pray

Never forget that from birth each child is a mixture of God's image and Adam's sin. Pray for families you know: ask the Lord to help parents raise children to know and fear the Lord.

Jealousy

Jealousy between brothers and sisters occurs in virtually every family. But although it is commonplace, it can become deadly serious…

Read Genesis 4:2-7

- ❓ *What does the passage tell us about God's response to the brothers and their offerings?*
- ❓ *What does it not tell us?*
- ❓ *What further information does Hebrews 11:4 provide?*

Cain falls out with Abel because he's jealous of his brother. Both of them bring offerings to God—Cain brings produce from the soil which he works, and Abel portions of first-born animals from his flocks. But there's something wrong! God, we are told, accepts "Abel and his offering", but not "Cain and his offering".

Genesis doesn't say why this is so, but Hebrews 11:4 helps: "By faith Abel brought God a better offering than Cain did". There's a difference of attitude between Cain and Abel. Cain's faithlessness becomes clear when he responds to God with anger, suggesting he felt he ought to have been accepted—that God, as it were, *owed him* acceptance, since Cain had been so good as to bring an offering.

A way out

- ❓ *What hope is there for Cain in Genesis 4:7?*
- ❓ *And what warning?*

God promises that Cain can still be accepted if he does "what is right" (v 7). This isn't yet

final rejection, only rebuke. God warns that sin's desire for Cain is like Eve's control-freakery towards Adam (compare 3:16b)! So he must resist. Failure to do "what is right" will lead to something far worse than has yet happened in human history.

⌄ Apply

Does Cain have free will? He certainly has *real* will—this is seen in how he made his offering, as well as his angry response to God's challenge. But can Cain turn himself from his chosen course of action? Despite God's warning, we can already foresee a tragic outcome.

- ❓ *What hope then is there for any of us? See Romans 8:1, 5-9.*

⌃ Pray

Beneath our polite and smooth exteriors, we are all a jumbled confusion of self-serving motives. It is a mistake to view Cain as a tragic failure that is unconnected with ourselves. Sin crouches at our door as well. So how can we resist its pull and instead "do what is right".

Read James 1:15 and Matthew 5:30

Use these verses to pray about the wrong desires you know you have.

Murder, he smote

The grim narrative plays itself out, as Cain plans and follows through on his jealous rage against his brother. But how will God respond?

Read Genesis 4:8-16

❓ *What do you think is the purpose of God's question in verse 9 (see 3:9)?*

Cain tries to hide the murder of Abel by inviting him for a walk in the countryside ("field" = "countryside" in Hebrew). But he can't avoid killing him in full view of God! Once again, the all-seeing God gives his sinful creature a chance to come clean, by asking Cain the whereabouts of his brother, just as he once asked Cain's dad: "Where are you?" (Genesis 3:9).

My brother's keeper?

❓ *How would you describe Cain's answer? And God's response to it?*

In view of what has happened, Cain's answer in 4:9 is astonishing—more like a sulky teenager dissing their parent than a sinner answering a direct question from almighty God. Yet even more astonishing is God's restraint in not destroying Cain immediately. Instead, he calls Cain to realise the enormity of his action. Cain claims ignorance, but Abel, though dead, "still speaks" (v 10; Hebrews 11:4). So once again, human sin invites God's curse (Genesis 4:11).

❓ *How is God's curse on Cain worse than that suffered by Adam (see 3:17-18)?*
❓ *How does God again temper his judgment with mercy?*

Earlier, the ground was cursed because of Adam (3:17). Now, Cain himself is cursed and completely alienated from the ground. For Adam it produced "thorns and thistles" (3:18) as well as food. Now it will yield nothing to Cain (4:12), who is therefore left to wander the earth. Note the connection between human sin and physical nature—creation groans because we sin (see Romans 8:20-22).

Yet the final surprise is that, despite Cain's lack of repentance, God's judgment is tempered with mercy. What Cain fears most—revenge—will not happen, for God puts a protective mark on him. Ultimately, vengeance belongs to God, not man (see Deuteronomy 32:35)

⌃ Pray

Inevitably, self-justification and hard-heartedness characterise those who are slaves to sin. Pray for yourself, that God would rid you of such sinful instincts.

Cain's legacy

The narrow focus of Genesis so far now broadens out to see how humanity spreads and grows. But it also charts the path of how sin spreads and grows…

Progress?

Read Genesis 4:17-18

Time moves on. Cain marries and settles down. Clearly, Cain is determined to secure a place for himself, for he names his "city" (which could be simply a village) after his own son. Perhaps, given his own past, he was wise not to name it "Cain".

The names of the next four generations (v 18) may reflect the character and hopes of this family line. Enoch means "dedicated" and Irad "swift". Mehujael means "smitten of God", and Methushael (probably) "man of God". But, finally, we come to Lamech ("powerful")—one of the Bible's most unsavoury characters.

Or degeneration?

Read Genesis 4:19-24

- ❓ *What is remarkable about this family?*
- ❓ *What is terrible about this family?*
- ❓ *What are the parallels between Cain's family and our modern world?*

Lamech is the first bigamist (v 19). The name of his first wife means "ornament", and he may indeed have treated her like a trophy. The other is Zillah, meaning "shade", and she was probably expected to live in his. However, they each have outstanding sons. Jabal and Jubal, the sons of Adah, are respectively the founders of animal husbandry and music (v 20-21). Tubal-cain, the son of Zillah, is the first engineer (v 22). Calvin rightly comments, "It is truly wonderful [= astonishing] that this race, which had most deeply fallen from integrity, should have excelled the rest of the posterity of Adam in rare endowments". One lesson is surely that true civilisation is not just a matter of knowledge, art and technology.

Lamech's character is revealed in his boast to his wives (v 23-24). Lamech avenges himself out of all proportion to the offence, or the ability of the offender to defend himself. Life in the Lamech household must have been miserable indeed. But there's one more bright note—his daughter's name, Naamah, means "pleasantness" or "loveliness". Perhaps she is another sign of God's mercy on sinners.

✓ Apply

Our culture abounds in technical skills and artistic creativity (both wonderful gifts of God), but without moral principles, and a Christian view of how gifts should be used to serve and bless others, the cycle of self-serving, power-wielding abuse will continue. Wonderful Christian families can produce faithless, determinedly destructive offspring. Utterly dissolute families can produce lovely individuals. It is a sign of the reality of sin and the way God is at work in the world.

Seth's line

The storyline in Genesis now rewinds to the time following Abel's murder.

Read Genesis 4:25 – 5:5

❓ *What is hopeful about Seth's birth (4:25)?*

❓ *What else is significant about Seth's arrival (5:3)?*

❓ *What further sign of hope can you find in these verses (4:26)?*

❓ *What shows that God's judgment remains inescapable (5:5)?*

Passing on the image

Adam and Eve's newborn son is seen as a replacement for Abel (4:25). His name, Seth, sounds like "appointed", because God has "granted" him in Abel's place. Adam's family tree in chapter 5 mentions neither Cain nor Abel, suggesting that the birth of Seth marks a fresh start.

But the start of what? Genesis 5:1-2 reminds us that man (*adam*) was made in the likeness and image of God. Seth is the son in Adam's own likeness and image (v 3)—a handed-down image of God.

Seth is not to be the final fulfilment of God's promise in Genesis 3:15. But he fathers Enosh. Enosh means "man", and so, as God called his image "man" (*adam*, 5:2)—God's image's image—Seth, also calls his son "man" (Enosh). God's image, though corrupted, is clearly being borne down this line.

Incidentally, both Eve and Adam are "man" (*adam*), according to 5:2, showing that male and female are fundamentally united as well as distinct.

Calling on the name

4:26 says that people "began to call on the name of the LORD"—which can mean to pray, but also to dedicate oneself to God, as Abraham did (Genesis 12:8; 21:33), and as all nations will do one day (Zephaniah 3:9). Meanwhile, God's curse on Adam is finally fulfilled—though he fathers many other children, he nevertheless dies (5:5).

⌃ Pray

"Everyone who calls on the name of the Lord will be saved." Romans 10:13

This is to be obeyed—in a life dedicated to God and lived in relationship with him—but also to be passed on to others...

Pray for opportunities today to do just that.

The generation game

Sometimes we can't avoid reading through genealogies. Unfortunately, there aren't many "blessed thoughts" in this one—or are there?

Read Genesis 5:6-32

- ❓ *Who does Seth's family line lead to?*
- ❓ *How does it compare with Cain's (4:17-24)?*
- ❓ *What pattern is repeated here?*
- ❓ *What truths does this genealogy emphasise?*

There's a rather depressing pattern here. Each person lives x years, fathers the next person in the genealogy, lives x years more, producing further children, has his lifespan totted up, and dies.

What's the point?

Three key features stand out.

1. This is real history. The story is told of a tribe who were unimpressed with the efforts of an evangelist until he showed them Bible genealogies. Suddenly, they began to pay attention. In their culture genealogies were taken seriously and this proved to them that the Bible was true. Certainly, Bible genealogies are always offered as completely serious records of family connections, to be taken at face value.

2. What matters is the line of descent. We've seen the line of Cain and how that ended with Lamech and his sons. Now we follow the line of Seth, and what matters is that it leads to Noah.

3. Everyone dies eventually. There's one exception to this rule—Enoch (5:21-24). After Methuselah's birth, Enoch did not merely "live", but "walked faithfully with God". And he did not die. Rather, "he was no more, because God took him away". What a marvellous and moving reminder of how life was surely meant to be—a walk with God and then going to be with him.

☑ Apply

Sin creates an inheritance of pain and further cruelty. But grace can break that cycle, and set whole families on a course of blessing that can have influence for generations to come.

- ❓ *How would you like future generations to look back on you?*

☑ Pray

Read Hebrews 11:5-6

- ❓ *What must Enoch have been like?*
- ❓ *What do you imagine it was like for him when God took him away? How might others have reacted?*

Pray that you may also walk faithfully with God.

Revive us

As we look around us at the state of church and nation, we are driven to thoughts and prayers like the ones we read today…

Read Psalm 85

❓ *What has God done in the past?*

❓ *What does the psalmist want to happen?*

❓ *How is God's character portrayed in the psalm?*

Like many of these psalms, this one begins with memories of God's past saving acts. Constantly through Israel's history, God had stepped in to rescue and restore his people. Rescue and restoration started with forgiveness because their plight was deserved —their punishment the result of God's righteous anger (v 1-3).

Now, the psalmist appeals to God. *Will you do the same again?* It's a plea that God will turn from his anger to forgive and so to revive a crushed, defeated and desperate people. Rescue and restoration are a result of God's "unfailing love". We can depend on his faithfulness and his loving character. The purpose of this "unfailing love" was to encourage worship: God's rescued people would be able to rejoice in him (v 4-7).

The psalmist chooses to listen to God and to hear what he has to say. He trusts God's promise that those who turn away from folly and towards God will know his peace and his presence (v 8-9). The song closes with an expression of confidence in God's character. In God, we see a meeting of love, faithfulness and righteousness. We ultimately see these things come together at the cross (v 10-13).

TIME OUT

Korah was one of the Levites during the exodus. He and some others rebelled and sought to usurp Moses and Aaron (Numbers 16) leading to judgment. His sons were spared and his descendants became responsible for tabernacle worship in the time of David. If they sung about being doorkeepers in God's house (Psalm 84) and God's power to forgive and restore, then they did so from personal experience.

❓ *How has your family's spiritual history shaped your walk with Christ?*

⌄ Apply

Are you downhearted at the state of the church in many places? Does it seem weak and compromised? Are you alert to the problem of sin in your own life? Do you feel distant from God at times? The promise of this psalm is that God is willing and able to forgive, cleanse and restore.

⌃ Pray

Many of us long to see revival in the church, but any such work needs to start in our own hearts. Take time to confess and repent where you have fallen and failed. Thank God that he is able and just to forgive you and to cleanse you.

Who were the Nephilim?

There is an odd feel about the language in today's passage that has provoked some wild speculation. Are these Neanderthals? Aliens? Or is there a more "ordinary" explanation?

Sons of God

Read Genesis 6:1-4

- ❓ *What's your impression of the behaviour of the "sons of God" in these verses?*
- ❓ *What is God's response?*
- ❓ *What clues are there to the identity of the "sons of God"? See also 5:1-3.*

Who are the "sons of God"? Here they are contrasted with the "daughters of humans". It's tempting to think that this is a contrast between angelic beings and humans. But perhaps the answer is rather more simple. God's response to their misbehaviour (5:3) suggests the sons of God are human. So, perhaps this is a contrast instead between more godly humans and their more worldly cousins.

We've already seen the human race divide into two lines—Cain's line, banished from the Lord's presence, but Seth's line representing a fresh start and carrying the "image" of God on from Adam. The most fitting explanation is that the "sons of God" are those of Seth's line, and the "daughters of men" are from outside this line. In 6:2, then, people in the supposedly godly line are being seduced by mere appearances— marrying whoever they "fancy", regardless of suitability.

In response, God puts a time limit on the first phase of human existence. ("120 years" probably refers to the approaching flood,

not man's lifespan.) The misbehaviour of the supposedly godly line shows that, at this stage, the Spirit's struggle with the flesh (NIV = "mortal", v 3) is not going to lead to real change in man.

⌄ Apply

Read Galatians 5:16-25

- ❓ *Where might you be in danger of compromising, because of an attraction to something that is beautiful but ungodly?*

The Nephilim

And who are the Nephilim (Genesis 6:4)? Again we might be tempted to think that this is some super-race of humanoids, but perhaps a simpler answer is more reasonable. They are described as mighty men of old—men with a name or reputation (see 11:4). They also appear later in history: the Anakites—terrifying enemies of Israel— were descended from them (see Numbers 13:33; Deuteronomy 1:27-29).

⌃ Pray

"You are all children of the light and children of the day. We do not belong to the night or to the darkness. So then, let us not be like others, who are asleep." 1 Thessalonians 5:5-6

Pray for those tempted to wander away from their heavenly Father—it may, of course, be you.

Grace and fervour

Don't imagine God had never noticed man's wickedness until now. Rather, the phrase "the LORD saw" shows he is about to take action.

Grim truth

Read Genesis 6:5-8

- ❓ *What is God's verdict on mankind?*
- ❓ *How does humanity's evil affect God?*
- ❓ *What is God's response to evil?*
- ❓ *What hope is there?*

God's verdict on mankind is devastating: "every inclination ... only evil all the time" (v 5). Mankind is incurably wicked to the core. This is the nature of sin—left unchecked it takes over, destroying the good like rust or a cancer. Verse 7 warns us chillingly of what God will do about this.

Understanding this corrosive viral effect of sin should help us understand why hell must be eternal. And motivate us to increasingly seek God's transforming grace in our lives (see 2 Corinthians 3:18).

Grief

What does Genesis 6:6 mean? Was God taken by surprise? Absolutely not, according to the rest of the Bible. Is this then just picture language—helping us understand God's deep opposition to evil, but corresponding to nothing in God himself? Ancient myths saw the gods as capricious and filled with rage—lashing out angrily in unpredictable ways. But here we see a very different picture. God is "grieved" by sin and the way mankind has turned out, but in a way that springs from his deep love for the world he created. He sheds tears over his ruined creatures.

Grace

But the story isn't over, and God hasn't yet revealed his complete purpose! Even now, there's a way ahead because "Noah found favour in the eyes of the LORD" (v 8). But this doesn't mean that Noah *deserved* salvation. In fact, to "find favour" is to receive more—sometimes much more—than one deserves (take a look at Esther 5:8; 4:11). Though Noah is described as righteous, he nevertheless receives mercy. And through him, so does the whole human race.

⌄ Apply

Be realistic about sinful nature—both yours and that of unbelievers, and other Christians. The fact that total depravity does not run rampant is only because of God's grace, shown in many ways—laws, conscience, timidity gaining the upper hand, plans frustrated and, ultimately, the gospel.

⌃ Pray

Thank God for his work in restraining sin, and for his grace in rescuing undeserving sinners.

Violence

God's purposes started with the first man, Adam, and people have grown and spread. Now, the focus comes down to a single man again: Noah.

Read Genesis 6:9-22

❓ *How is Noah described in these verses?*
❓ *How are all other people described?*
❓ *What does God promise will be destroyed (v 13, 17)?*
❓ *What does God promise will continue (v 18-20)?*

"Un-creation"

The whole world is "corrupt ... and ... full of violence" (v 11). "Violence" here implies cruelty. The result of unchecked sin is that the earth becomes totally "corrupt" (v 11-12). As Romans 8:19-22 shows, creation itself is affected by man's sin. So God resolves on a plan of virtual "un-creation". He will destroy both corrupt mankind and the corrupted earth (Genesis 6:13).

🔼 Pray

It feels as if the earth is still "full of violence". What has changed since the days of Noah? **Read Matthew 24:37-39.**

Pray for victims of violence—and also for their oppressors.

Salvation

Yet it's not the end of the story. Noah, his family, and with them, every kind of living organism on earth, will be saved. Noah is to build an ark (Genesis 6:14-16)—something

more like a coffin than the boat beloved of children's books. Destruction by a flood of waters will bring back the situation of Genesis 1:2.

Re-creation

Then God promises to "establish" his covenant with Noah (6:18), an expression which suggests continuing an existing arrangement rather than creating something new. God is not abandoning what he began in Genesis 1, but only bringing an end to the accelerating downward spiral of sin which has been happening since Genesis 3. There will be a fresh start for all life, and so every type of living creature is to be preserved (v 19-21), not just the human race.

🔽 Apply

❓ *In what ways are Noah's world and ours similar? In what ways are they different?*

Noah was different from those around him, as we expect from someone with biblical faith. But it was Noah's obedience to God's command (v 22) that was the act of faith crucial to his salvation. His obedience brought with it hard work, mockery and the misunderstanding of many. But by persevering, he was saved, along with his family

❓ *Is that the pattern of believing life you are leading?*

Drowning by numbers

After a long time of preparation, the fateful day arrived when the storm clouds gathered and the rain started to fall.

Read Genesis 7:1-16 and 2 Peter 2:5

❷ *How does Peter describe Noah? Why, do you think?*

❷ *What is repeated three times in these verses? Compare with Genesis 6:22.*

The day of salvation

Building the ark must have taken many years and during that time Noah's neighbours would have wondered what was going on. Noah's "ridiculous" project stood as a warning to the people of his generation. It must have created many opportunities for them to hear about the coming judgment. But they did not repent, and the day came when only he, his family, and the animals went into the ark (7:1).

Despite the indifference and rejection, Noah had persevered. Genesis underlines again (v 5, 9, and 16) that his obedience to God's word was crucial. Peter calls Noah a "herald/preacher of righteousness" (2 Peter 2:5). And God himself tells Noah that he finds him to be righteous!

🔽 Apply

Read 2 Peter 3:3-7, 11-12

❷ *Are you willing to accept ridicule for your obedience to God's word?*

Pray for "preachers of righteousness"

you know to persevere, and for ears to be opened, hearts softened, and people saved.

The day of judgment

Seven days are allowed to get everyone and everything into the ark—a deliberate parallel perhaps of the seven days of creation—and then the flood begins. The specific dating and timings of the flood (Genesis 7:11) shows that this writer meant it to be seen as a fixture on the calendar. Water comes from above and below (compare v 11 with 1:2), as the divisions created in 1:6-10 are undone.

Noah and his family are last into the ark (7:13) and God himself closes the door (v 16). There's a touching intimacy here—God doesn't stand aloof from what is happening, but, even at this early stage, involves himself in the process of salvation.

🔼 Pray

Life went on "as normal" for most people while Noah prepared the ark (see Luke 17:26-27). Perhaps, instead of praying for peace, we should pray instead for upheavals to shake people today out of their complacency.

And pray for opportunities to share the news of the coming judgment, and God's gracious provision of an "ark" in Jesus.

Judgment falls

Picture the ark alone on a waterscape that stretched to the horizon in all directions. Safely tucked away inside are Noah, his family and a vast menagerie of creatures.

Read Genesis 7:1-24

❓ *List all the details about the flood given in this chapter.*

-
-
-
-
-
-
-

❓ *What are the implications of doubting that the flood was a real event (see 7:4)?*

The precise description of the flood given here is intended to show that this was a real event. As God promised (v 4), the rain lasts forty days, during which time every land animal and bird outside the ark perishes.

⌄ Apply

Peter refers to the flood when warning Christians against listening to those who scoff at God's promise of judgment (2 Peter 3:3-7).

❓ *Think about what the flood was like, both for those inside and outside the ark.*
❓ *How will this motivate you today?*

Re-creation
Read Genesis 8:1-22

When destruction is completed, God is moved to act (v 1). The waters recede and the ark grounds. The description of the slow drying process (v 2-5) further emphasises these events were real.

❓ *Why were seven of each clean animal taken into the ark (7:2)?*
❓ *What do God's words in 8:17 remind us of?*
❓ *What two intentions does God express (v 21)? Despite what?*

Noah makes preparations to leave the ark (v 6-14), but God gives the final "all clear" (v 15-17). At this point, God's words clearly echo Genesis 1:22 and 28. Life will again multiply and fill the earth—this is "re-creation".

Extra clean animals were needed on the ark so Noah could make sacrifices to the Lord (8:20). This pleases God (v 21)—a right relationship with God always involves appropriate sacrifice (compare 4:4; Hebrews 9:22b). This is the context in which God shows mercy, promising no further curse on the ground, or total destruction of life while the earth endures—even though man's heart hasn't changed (Genesis 8:21b; compare 6:5).

Nevertheless, the New Testament warns us judgment still awaits—but next time by fire not water (see 2 Peter 3:6-7).

❓ *How will you make a pleasing sacrifice to God today?*

The curse continues

After the flood there's a new beginning for life on earth, and God again repeats his command about multiplying and filling the earth.

A new hope
Read Genesis 9:1-17

> ❷ *Compare verses 1-3 and 1:28-30. What important change is mentioned?*
> ❷ *What command shows that all life is precious?*
> ❷ *Why is human life of ultimate value?*

Noah (the name sounds like "comfort" in Hebrew) was so named in the hope he would be a "comforter" regarding God's curse of the ground (5:28-29). God now eases that curse by allowing mankind to eat meat (9:2-3). However, life remains precious, so meat must not be eaten with the "lifeblood" still in it (v 4). And human life is of ultimate value because, despite the fall, humankind is still the image of God (v 5-6). So any animal or human being who takes human life forfeits their own.

A continuing covenant

> ❷ *What promises does God make?*
> ❷ *How are they the same, yet different from earlier covenants made by God?*

God sets his intentions for creation (8:21-22) into a covenant (9:8-11). The rainbow becomes a sign that the covenant will always be honoured (v 12-17). When God "remembers" his covenant (v 15), it doesn't mean he otherwise forgets it, but that he will act on it.

A moral collapse
Read Genesis 9:18-29

> ❷ *What do you find so tragic about Noah's drunkenness and what follows?*

But instead of a bright new future, tragically, Noah now reveals his human weakness (v 20-21). His naked drunkenness is bad enough, but worse follows, when Ham encourages his two brothers to mock their father (v 22), though unsuccessfully. When Noah discovers the truth, disaster follows. Having been mocked by his son, he underlines the terrible gravity of disrespecting a parent by cursing his son's son. Ironically, the great hope for relief from God's curse hands down a curse himself (v 25).

At the end of the story of the flood, the pattern of chapter 5 is repeated: "Noah lived a total of 950 years, and then he died" (v 28-29). Sin has been restrained but not defeated, and death still reigns. It feels like we are back to pre-flood life so quickly.

☑ Apply

Even great saints may have a great fall. Take 1 Corinthians 10:12 to heart today.

My greatest need

We are so wrapped up in the visceral details of our immediate problems that it can take a huge effort to stand back and see the wider picture. David will help us...

Read Psalm 86

- ❓ *On what basis does David cry out to God?*
- ❓ *How does God compare to other gods?*
- ❓ *What two things does David ask for from God (v 2, 11)?*
- ❓ *What is God like and how does this help David to face his enemies?*

In among the psalms of Asaph and the Korahites, we find a prayer from David also petitioning God for help. David bases his request on three things:

- his own poverty and need (v 1),
- his trust in the faithful God (v 2, 4), and
- that he is calling out to God (v 3).

He can trust God and cry out to him when in need because of what God is like. The Lord is forgiving, good and loving (v 5-7). This distinguishes the Lord from all other gods. He is the true and living God who acts to save. He alone is worthy of praise (v 8-10).

David recognises that his greatest need, even in the face of threat from fearsome enemies, is to know God better. So, David's first prayer is that God will change his heart. He asks for an undivided heart. In other words, he asks the Lord to help him to be loyal and faithful to God alone without distraction or having a rival for his affections (v 11-13).

This is not to deny or ignore David's immediate need and danger. God is not disinterested in our daily lives. David does face real enemies. However, David does not need to fear them because he knows who God is and what he is like. God is loving, gracious, patient and trustworthy, so, he asks God to give a sign, or evidence, of these characteristics, so that his enemies might see and know (v 14-17).

⌄ Apply

Whatever you might be facing today, your greatest need is for a fresh vision of who God is and a deeper grasp of the gospel. It is remembering these great truths—that God is love and that he has forgiven and redeemed you—which will keep you going through whatever trials you might be facing.

⌃ Pray

Ask God to help you with the specific circumstances you are facing today. Pray that even through your trials and struggles, God would work in your life to change your heart and to grow your love for him and trust in him.

Pray the prayers of verses 2 and 11 for yourself and those you love.

Life goes on (and down)

Old Testament genealogies can appear a bit dull and irrelevant to us. But, like scaffolding, they provide a framework for understanding other parts of the Bible story.

Continuation

The value of family history isn't just that it satisfies curiosity about where we've come from—it also shows something vitally important about who we are...

Read Genesis 10

> ❓ *How do these verses show the unity and diversity of all people?*
> ❓ *How does Paul pick this up evangelistically in Acts 17:26-27?*

Genesis 10 shows how the human race developed from one man, Noah, but along many different branches. Interestingly, exactly 70 of Noah's descendants are mentioned here—a good symbolic biblical number indicating "the totality" of all nations on earth. It gives the clue that what we are reading here is probably not the whole story, but a structured list designed to make a point. One branch would be crucial in God's plan of salvation for the world.

···· TIME OUT ·······································

Read 1 Corinthians 9:19-23

> ❓ *What challenge does the diversity of the human race present to Christians seeking to spread the gospel?*
> ❓ *Why is it important to understand that all humans originate from one man?*

Read John 1:9

Generations

The chapter traces the descendants of each of Noah's sons in turn. From Japheth came several groups including the maritime nations (Genesis 10:5). Among Ham's descendants, Nimrod stands out (v 9), but his legacy—the cities of Babylon and Nineveh—would later bring great suffering to Israel.

The one to watch...

That would be Shem. The line of Shem's grandson, Eber (v 21, 24), is highlighted. Here, only Peleg (meaning "split") is singled out for mention. Verse 25 probably refers to the division of earth's languages. Despite mention of Joktan's line (v 26-28), Peleg's descendants are the ones to watch (check out Luke 3:23-38). No reason is given why Shem's line was chosen over his brothers' descendants—it's God's sovereign grace at work.

⌃ Pray

Human divisions lie behind almost all conflicts. The "gospel answer" is not a fake tolerance but unity in and through Christ. Christians can rejoice in their diversity.

Pray for this "diverse unity" among Christians you know, and for your witness to those different from you.

Towering talk

Language is a fantastic thing, distinguishing us from animals and allowing us to relate to God.

Yet, although our brains are "hard-wired" to develop language as we grow, there are no "innate" human words—they all have to be learned. Language seems to exist "outside" us. At first the human race shared one common language. But this was to change dramatically.

Rebellion

Read Genesis 11:1-9

❷ *What were the ultimate aims of building this city and tower (v 4)?*

Compare what God says to Abraham in Genesis 12:2. And his instruction to Noah in 9:1.

❷ *So what was wrong with these aims?*

The language of pride

Mankind planned to become a self-made entity which would inevitably worship itself as its own "creator". The city/tower and the name they would make for themselves would keep the race together as it expanded (11:4). But the notion that mankind could define itself in its own terms is revealed as godless arrogance and comes under God's judgment.

The early chapters of Genesis present a pattern of human failure and divine grace. Each of God's judgments is tempered with mercy.

❷ *How has God both judged and shown mercy to Adam and Eve, then to Cain, and finally to the whole human race?*

But now mercy seems to be withheld...

Read Genesis 11:1-9 again

Trashing talk

❷ *What does God do before he judges?*
❷ *What are God's motives for this?*

God's judgment is not from jealousy of humanity's power and independence. God investigates before he judges (v 5). He sees that a fallen but united humanity will be unrestrained in potential for evil (v 6). Confusing their language confounds their plan (v 7-8). So judgment is an act of love and mercy for humankind. They will not be subjected to the evils that a single unitary culture can bring. The word "Babel" (v 9) sounds like the Hebrew for "confused". Babylon, the "city of confusion", will remain throughout Scripture as a symbol of human and spiritual opposition to God.

⌃ Pray

In Revelation 18 we read about the end of Babylon, and all who "live" there. Pray for yourself and your church, to always live for God's everlasting kingdom, not for the fading pleasures of this broken and compromised world.

Introducing Abram

It's another genealogy, and once again the line of Shem is highlighted. But this list takes us on further—to a person and an event crucial to God's plan of salvation.

Who

Read Genesis 11:10-32

Shem's descendants as far as Peleg have been listed before (10:22-25). Now we learn about five more generations down to Terah (11:24), who becomes the new focus (v 27). Terah has three sons—Abram, Nahor and Haran, but, after fathering Lot, Haran dies (significantly) "in the land of his birth" (v 28). Nahor marries his niece by Haran, and Abram marries Sarai, who is barren (v 30)—a problem which will haunt Abram for the next several decades. The name Abram means "exalted father"—or in popular culture "Big Daddy". The name has a deep irony to it, which would be filled with pain for the childless Abram and Sarai.

> ❷ *Why do you think Abram is introduced here, directly after the story of Babel? (Clue: what was missing from that account of God's judgment?)*

In Genesis so far, God has always tempered judgment with mercy. After Babel, God judged mankind by dividing the world into different nations. Now he begins the process of building one of those nations to become the vessel of his greatest mercy to all nations. This passage gives us the back story of people who might be seen as rather irrelevant in the big sweep of history, but who will be hugely significant in God's story of salvation.

Where

Nahor and the family of Haran remain behind in Ur (see 22:23; 24:4), while Abram, his wife, father and nephew set out for Canaan. But Terah only gets as far as the town called Harran, where he dies aged 205.

Why

The family first left for Canaan under the leadership of Terah. However, it appears that this journey was made because of God's command specifically to Abram (12:1, "The LORD *had* said to Abram..."). The Bible's focus is on Abram and concludes that he "obeyed" (see Hebrews 11:8).

☑ Apply

We must be careful not to whitewash the towering figures of these patriarchs. Abram's family were idolaters (read Joshua 24:14), and we will see clearly Abram's moral weakness and failure in the chapters ahead.

> ❷ *So why did God choose him?*

⌃ Pray

Obedience is the heartbeat of faith. God chooses just an ordinary man, an ordinary family. Pray that your own family may be obedient to God and therefore useful to him in achieving his purposes in the world.

The call

Today's short reading is utterly crucial and foundational for our understanding of the Bible story. It's not too bold to say that the rest of the Bible rests on these three verses.

Read Genesis 12:1-3

God's call came to Abram before he reached Haran—he had already left his country, people and father's household (12:1) and was on route to Canaan (11:31; Acts 7:1-2). These verses here underline how Abram's call is a crucial moment in the Bible's story—the turning point in God's dealings with mankind. Until now, there has been a cycle of sin, judgment and mercy, and nothing has disrupted that pattern. The curses pronounced in Genesis 3 have shown no signs of being lifted. Even after the flood, Noah's family still carried the effects of the fall. Now, however, there is a promise of something radically different...

Blessings *for* Abram

❓ *What specific promises does God make to Abram in Genesis 12:2-3?*
❓ *How would they transform Abram's life?*
❓ *Like so many since, Abram is a migrant in search of a better life. But what is different about Abram's motives?*

Abram was a stateless nomad—but he would be brought to the land promised to him. Abram was childless—but through a family of his own he would become a great nation. Abram was unknown—but he would have a great name (see 11:4). He sets out on this journey not simply for a better, blessed life, but in response to the promises and call of God.

Blessings *through* Abram

❓ *Who would receive blessings through Abram? Why?*
❓ *Who wouldn't receive blessings through Abram?*

Abram himself would be a blessing to others. It wasn't a matter of using Abram's name to invoke blessing. Rather, he would be the deciding factor in God's own blessing—God would act according to how people responded to Abram.

And ultimately, Abram would become the source of blessing to "all peoples on earth". "Peoples" can also be translated "families". This wouldn't be a tribal blessing, limited to Abram's group and those who join it, but a global blessing. The rest of the Bible shows the unfolding of this promise. But at the close of the Old Testament, how the nations will be blessed is yet to be revealed.

⌄ Apply

God makes an obscure, stateless nomad, stricken with childlessness, into a conduit for his purposes for all mankind! Abram, despite lapses into weakness and sinfulness (see following chapters), responds with obedience (12:4). The lesson to us is obvious.

❓ *Are you going to have an obedient day today?*

Challenges and curses

The Bible doesn't show us "plaster saints"—quite the reverse. Today, we see Abram living in self-sacrificial obedience, quickly followed by his acting like a total scumbag.

Read Genesis 12:4-20

❷ *What encouragements does Abraham receive during his travels (v 5, 7)?*
❷ *What challenges does he face (v 6, 10)?*
❷ *How does verse 8 reveal his faith?*
❷ *How do verses 10-13 reveal the limits of Abraham's faith?*

The story picks up from 11:32—Abram continues towards Canaan. Note how the family have prospered in Haran (12:5). God is already blessing Abraham richly, and yet, he continues the journey into the unknown—leaving wealth, stability, peace and comfort, based just on a word of promise from God.

Dedication

Arriving in Canaan, Abram is told that this is the land God has promised him. However, it's already populated. Abram builds an altar to the Lord (v 7). Further on in his travels through the land, he builds a second altar and calls on the name of the Lord (v 8). This phrase (see 4:26), coupled with altar-building, indicates Abram's deliberate dedication of himself and the land to God.

Deception

But then things take a turn for the worse—there's famine (12:10). And although Abram has obeyed God's call, there are limits to his trust. To escape the famine, Abram moves to Egypt. Anxious that jealousy of his beautiful wife will result in his murder there, Abram instructs Sarai to hide the truth about their marriage (v 13).

❷ *How does what happens to Abram, Sarai and Pharaoh show God's promises in verses 1-3 in action?*

Things appear to work out. Sarai is "acquired" by Pharaoh but Abram is treated well "for her sake" (v 16). Yet something isn't right. Abram, the channel of God's blessing to the world, is blessed because of Sarai. On the other hand, Pharaoh is cursed because of her (v 17), despite his innocence in this matter (v 18-19)! Abram's deception means that the programme of world blessing has not started well.

❷ *Why do you think Pharaoh was cursed by God, even though he had "blessed" Abram?*

✓ Apply

God is doing his gospel work of blessing the world even through the worst and most damaging behaviour of his people. How have you seen this happening in your own life, church or ministry?

^ Pray

Our faith shines brightest when it is dangerous to believe: pray that you will learn to trust God, even in circumstances where faithfulness to him might prove costly.

Hard choices

Having been thrown out of Egypt, Abram returns to the southern part of Canaan, where his faith in God's promises is tested once again. How will he respond?

Family therapy

Read Genesis 13:1-13

❓ *Where does Abram return to (v 3) and what does he do there?*

❓ *What might this reveal about his spiritual state?*

❓ *Look at Abram's response to the next crisis (v 5-8). How does he show greater maturity?*

A nomad once more, Abram returns to the altar at Bethel and again calls on the name of the Lord (v 4). In Hebrew, the word for "repentance" means to "return", and there's a note of penitence in this return to Bethel. Soon we discover how Abram has matured —he approaches the next crisis with a much more obvious trust in God.

Testing times

The wealth Abram and Lot gained in Egypt means the land simply cannot support all their flocks (v 5-7). The obvious thing is for Abram and Lot to separate. And clearly, since God has promised the land to Abram, he should have first choice. But instead, Abram gives the first choice to Lot (v 8-9).

Abram could be accused of giving away the land God had promised him—something for which Esau would later be judged (see Genesis 25:29-34).

❓ *Why was it an act of faith to give Lot first choice?*

A dangerous decision

❓ *What drove Lot's decision (13:10)?*

❓ *What motivated him?*

❓ *What did he choose to ignore (v 13)?*

Understandably, but dangerously, Lot chose the best land, and separated from Abram (v 11). Yet the evidence of his eyes (compare v 3 and v 6) and his eagerness to take the best land misled Lot, for Sodom was a place opposed to God himself (v 13). This must have become obvious to Lot as he got to know the area, and yet he set up camp near Sodom itself (v 12). Lot was courting spiritual, moral, and—ultimately—physical disaster.

🔺 Pray

❓ *In what areas of your life might you have pitched your own tent "near Sodom"?*

Pray for yourself and others you know who are taking unnecessary spiritual risks.

The glorious city

There are lots of popular songs in praise of cities: New York, New York; In my Liverpool home; I belong to Glasgow. This is a song in praise of God's city.

Read Psalm 87

❓ *How does the psalmist speak of Zion/Jerusalem?*

❓ *Who else acknowledges God?*

❓ *Why is there a special blessing for those born within Zion's walls?*

This psalm focuses on Zion, or Jerusalem— God's city as the place that is central to his purposes and promises (v 1). The city has been founded and established by God: it is his own city. He loves the city and it is of greatest importance among all of the towns and cities of the land (v 2).

Zion is praised as glorious (v 3). People tell of its greatness and special status. The psalmist envisages a day when the nations around will come to acknowledge the true God. He lists Egypt, Philistia, Tyre, Cush. But notice that they are described as *being born* in Zion. Insofar as they come to acknowledge God, it is because of Jerusalem (v 4-5). This ties into prophecies which speak about the nations being drawn to Jerusalem to learn about the living God (see Micah 4 for example). There was something significant, something unique, about being born in the city. It is a special privilege (Psalm 87:6-7).

TIME OUT

Rahab, not to be confused with the woman who gave refuge to spies in Jericho, was the name of a mythical sea monster. It seems also to have been used as a nickname for

Egypt. So verse 4 is a list of the enemies of Israel and how they come to acknowledge the privilege of those who are sons of Zion.

☑ Apply

We must apply all the psalms through a New Testament lens. If there is a particular blessing to being born within the walls of Zion/Jerusalem, then who does that apply to now? In Revelation 21:1-4, John describes a vision of the new Jerusalem coming down to earth. This is the bride of Christ. In other words, Jerusalem represents God's people, the church.

Those who are born and registered there then, are those whose names are written in the lamb's book of life. To be born within Zion's walls means to be someone who has been born again and, through faith in Jesus Christ, become part of God's people. Our concern then should be to see many of our friends and neighbours able to say that they have experienced this new birth.

︿ Pray

Think of three people who you would love to see experience new birth and so become part of the new Jerusalem. Take a moment to pray for them and for gospel opportunities now.

Read (or sing) the words of the hymn *Glorious things of thee are spoken*.

 Bible in a year: Psalms 120 – 122 • 2 Corinthians 6

Confirmation bias

Abram has let Lot take first pick of the land. Lot, like Eve, has followed his eyes and opted for what looks good, regardless of the spiritual danger involved.

....

Read Genesis 13:14-18

Lot's choice

- ❓ *How might Abram be feeling when Lot leaves him with the leftovers?*
- ❓ *What difference would God's words to him make (v 14-17)?*

Had Abram made a huge mistake in letting Lot pick the best land? No! Because now God tells him to do what Lot had done: "Look around from where you are" (v 14). But whereas Lot looked and chose just one area, Abram is told to look "north and south, to the east and west", because *all* this land is for him and his offspring for ever (v 15). God is reaffirming the promise given in 12:1-3.

God's promise

- ❓ *What additional detail of his promise does God now reveal?*
- ❓ *How might this be both comforting but also depressing for Abram (hint: what does his name mean)?*

Abram was told he would be "a great nation" (12:2a). Now he learns just how great—his offspring will be uncountable (13:16). Just because Lot has bagged the best land, the promise of God has not been threatened.

- ❓ *What does God want Abram to do with his gift?*

God tells Abram to "walk through the length and breadth of the land" (v 17a), because it's all his as a gift from God (v 17b). The right response is to rejoice and delight in God's generosity.

☑ Apply

- ❓ *What gifts of God do you truly revel in— or do you just intellectually accept them in a rather dry way?*
- ❓ *How could you "walk through the length and breadth" of the gospel life you have been given?*

Abram's altar

Abram built a third altar to the Lord at Hebron—he knew that a relationship with God involves a costly sacrifice, though he didn't yet know how costly it could be.

☒ Pray

As believers today, we understand more clearly the cost of grace. The cross not only reveals how horrific our sins are but also how greatly God is offended by them. But God wants us to be *penitent* sinners, not *abject* sinners.

After you have prayed in sorrow, rejoice in his restoration, and determine to enjoy today the wonderful "land" you have been given.

Rescue party

Perhaps Abram imagined life would become more straightforward from now on. But he and his family are now caught up in a conflict which was not of their own making.

A bigger picture

Read Genesis 14:1-16

Chapter 14 introduces us to the political background, and to what would dog Israel for the rest of her history—although the land was promised, it needed to be possessed and the other residents would not move out easily, and external forces are ever present. Four powerful kings from the east oppress the land, but five local kings rebel, including those of Sodom and Gomorrah.

The year following the uprising, the four overlords take to the field, sweeping down the east side of the Jordan to the Red Sea, then back up through the Negev to the southern border of the rebels' territory (v 5-7). The rebels make a stand but are defeated (v 8-9). In the rout, some of the vanquished are trapped in the local tar pits, while others escape to the hills (v 10).

❓ *Where is Lot now living (v 12)?*
❓ *What is the consequence of this?*
❓ *Where is Abram living (v 13)*
❓ *How is it now seen as a blessing that Abram did not choose the best land?*

Abram to the rescue

All this upheaval would have quite literally passed Abram by but for one thing. In the looting of Sodom and Gomorrah, Lot—now living in, not just near, Sodom—is captured along with some of the local inhabitants.

However, Abram has three allies (v 13) and a substantial force of "trained men" (v 14). He leads the pursuit and launches a coordinated night attack from several directions (v 15a), showing remarkable combat skills. The enemy is routed and Abram returns with all the rescued captives, including Lot.

Abram was godly, but militarily he was also prudent—he had over 300 "trained" men and an alliance with three local brothers.

❓ *Where might you or your church need to make prudent plans to get ready for unforeseen future problems?*
❓ *What training might be good to do now for yourself, your children or other believers you know?*
❓ *How will you keep them within a context of overall trust in God?*

···· TIME OUT ······················

Note that the sword can never set up the kingdom of God (see Matthew 26:52; John 18:36), but God uses it to punish wrongdoers (Romans 13:4) and enact his will.

❓ *When might it be right to use force?*

⌃ Pray

Pray for wisdom for Christians worldwide, caught up in the sweep of world events like this. Pray that they would have courage, wisdom and act decisively and faithfully.

Two kingdoms

After his victorious rescue mission, Abram is greeted by two different "kings". But their attitude, and his response to them, are strangely different.

Dividing the loot

Read Genesis 14:17-24

❓ *Which two kings greet Abram on his return from the rescue mission?*

❓ *How does Abram respond to each?*

❓ *What are we told about Melchizedek?*

❓ *Compare verse 19 with 12:3. What is strange here?*

❓ *Why do you think Abram reacted so differently to the two kings?*

The king of Sodom must have survived the fighting (unless it's a new king), and greets the returning Abram (14:17). But another king is present—Melchizedek, king of Salem (v 18). His name means "My King is Righteousness", and his town's name is "Peace". And he is mysteriously resonant of other parts of the Bible.

First, this king brings with him bread and wine, rather than the more usual bread and water (e.g. Deuteronomy 23:4) This seems celebratory, not merely charitable. More curiously, he is also a priest—"of God Most High" (Genesis 14:18). Melchizedek recognises this God as Creator (v 19) and knows that he has acted on Abram's behalf (v 20). Abram too recognises this is indeed his God (v 22).

The blesser blessed!

But strangest of all is that, despite the promise of Genesis 12:1-3, it's Melchizedek who blesses Abram (14:19), the one through whom blessing is to come. And Abram recognises that Melchizedek is worthy to do this by giving him a tenth of his plunder (v 20).

An atmosphere of awe surrounds Melchizedek. Not surprisingly, the Old Testament associates him with the Messiah (see Psalm 110:4) and the New Testament recognises him as a foreshadowing of Christ (see Hebrews 5:6-10; 7:1-22).

By contrast, Abram rejects the king of Sodom's offer of compensation (Genesis 14:21-22)—there's no way the king of Sodom will be able to say he did anything for Abram, no matter how deserved it was (v 23).

⌄ Apply

Apparently Abram recognises the character of the king of Sodom, and scrupulously stays out of his debt. Sometimes we are called to do the same.

⌃ Pray

Spend time in praise of Christ, the true King and Priest "in the order of Melchizedek".

Check your credit score

At some unspecified time after the previous incidents, "The word of the LORD came to Abram". What is revealed has massive implications for him, and for us.

Vast vision

Read Genesis 15:1-6

- ❓ What is Abram not to do? Why?
- ❓ But what is Abram's great fear?
- ❓ How does God respond to Abram's initial disregard of his message?
- ❓ What's the turning point here in the Bible's revelation of how to be right with God?

God's message—*I am your protection and your recompense*—is doubtless reassuring, but, the way Abram sees it, this doesn't tell him what he really wants to know. Verse 2 is a cry from the heart—*That's all very well, but what good is it to a childless man whose only heir is his servant?*

There's a caution here for Christians offering spiritual comfort to those burdened by their immediate needs. It may be true to say to the childless, the lonely, the jobless or the widowed, "Don't worry, you have the Lord", but that doesn't automatically alleviate their pain. Notice God doesn't criticise Abram for his "short-sightedness". Instead, he addresses his "felt need" through another message. Abram's own son will be his heir (v 4). And what's more, his offspring will be as countless as the stars on a clear desert night (v 5).

Apply

- ❓ What genuine comfort can we offer those who are facing immediate pain and need, and for whom God seems very distant and even absent?

Right by faith

Verse 6 is a turning point in biblical theology. Paul quotes it to show that Abr(ah)am was justified by faith, not works (Romans 4:1-3, 22). This isn't the moment of Abram's "conversion"—he is already God's faithful servant, chosen by grace. But we see here what true faith really is—a belief in God through his word. And we see what our gracious God does for those who demonstrate genuine faith. Abram now trusts the God who has spoken, and so responds to him as he should. A right relationship exists between God and Abram—there is "righteousness", based on grace and faith.

Pray

Christian faith is not "believing the impossible" but believing God; not persuading yourself about future events but trusting a person. And it's a gift from God (Ephesians 2:8).

Ask God to give you deeper trust in him and his word of promise in Christ.

Cutting a covenant

One way of "sealing a deal" in the ancient world was for participants to sacrifice an animal and walk together between the separated parts.

The deal makers are saying: *may I too be chopped up if I break this contract!*

Read Genesis 15:7-21

❷ *What does Abram need reassurance about now?*

Verse 6 seems to be a comment for the reader, not a reflection of Abram's own awareness, since in verse 7 he is still seeking reassurance—this time about the land. His question in verse 8 parallels his question in verse 2.

What follows in verses 9-19 is a solemn covenant ceremony performed in a familiar way that Abram would understand. God binds *himself* to his word. But verse 6 tells us that Abram's righteousness in relation to God is established by trust in his word alone, not by relying on the guarantee given by the covenant ceremony, however important that is.

God cuts a deal

The verb used to describe "making" a covenant is literally "to cut". Abram is told to assemble sacrificial animals (v 9), and to cut all except the two birds in two, arranging the halves with space between them (v 10). When dusk falls, God speaks to Abram as he sleeps (v 12).

❷ *What's the bad news?*
❷ *What's the good news?*

❷ *Why so long before Abram's descendants will possess the land (see v 16)?*
❷ *What part does Abram take in this sacred covenant cutting?*

First, God tells Abram the painful future awaiting his descendants. Only after 400 years of mistreatment in another land will they even begin to take possession of the land where Abram now sits (v 13). This is because possession of the land by his people must await the time when the present inhabitants truly deserve dispossession because of their sins (v 16). But deliverance and justice will eventually come (v 14).

Jeremiah 34:18-19 explains the significance of Abram's strange vision in Genesis 15:17. Walking between the halves of the animals invoked either blessing for obedience to what was being promised, or a curse for disobedience. But only God does this—Abram is still sound asleep. God takes on himself alone responsibility for the consequences of covenant-breaking—a commitment that would finally be fulfilled at the cross.

⌃ Pray

Thank God for his total commitment to us, and his love, which bears the consequences of our sin.

A helping hand?

Perhaps you sometimes secretly feel that God needs a hand—like Saraï. It's an almost certain recipe for disaster…

Read Genesis 16:1-6

- ❷ *How does Saraï see God at work (v 2)?*
- ❷ *What does she fail to do (see 15:4)?*
- ❷ *How does this story reflect what happened in Eden (3:6, 17)?*
- ❷ *What are the consequences?*

When God made his promise to Abram in precise and emphatic detail (15:4), he knew that Saraï was infertile. But whatever condition someone is in when they're called, that's surely good enough for God (see 1 Corinthians 7:7-24).

Saraï's impatience comes from a fundamental mistrust in God's word. She sees God at work, but only negatively (Genesis 16:2). So, like Abram earlier (12:11-13), she plans to move things along. Saraï's servant can act as a surrogate mother. Yes, Hagar is an Egyptian, but the child will surely be as good as Saraï's own.

That fatal "Yes, dear"

Abram's response (16:2) is more than mere agreement. The Hebrew phrasing means that he "obeyed" his wife—just as Adam "listened to" Eve (3:17). There are also echoes of 2:21-22 when Saraï presents Hagar to Abram (16:3). Just like Eve, Saraï has reversed the God-given roles in marriage, and has not taken God at his word. Despite God's promise, the best Abram can manage is a "Yes, dear".

But, as in Eden, the plan backfires horribly. Hagar promotes herself to "Number One Wife" (v 4), and Saraï (naturally) blames Abram (v 5). Unsurprisingly, Abram washes his hands of the whole affair. Saraï is allowed to vent her spleen on the unfortunate Hagar. Abram, meanwhile, was no doubt lying low in the patriarchal equivalent of the garden shed.

☑ Apply

Abram was a man of faith (15:6), but found it especially hard to live out his faith at home.

- ❷ *Why is the home such a tough spiritual battleground?*

We need people to be practical in spiritual things, but there can be a danger that pragmatism takes over.

- ❷ *How can we ensure that we are also spiritual in practical things?*

◤ Pray

Pray about your own "domestic" life, whatever that is. Ask that your faith will follow you home, and that mere pragmatism will not rule your decision making.

My closest friend

We often speak of "the dark night of the soul". Here is a glimpse into one writer's darkest fears; but there is another hidden and glorious depth to this song…

Read Psalm 88

❓ *Where does the psalmist find himself?*
❓ *Who does he think has done this to him? Why?*
❓ *Where is hope in the passage?*

This psalm starts with a plea to God for salvation (v 1-2). Here, the songwriter vividly describes what it feels like to be brought to your lowest ebb. He is overwhelmed by trouble. He is like someone cast into the pit, both a reference to an individual tomb and to Sheol or Hades. The implication is that he feels as though he belongs with the dead (v 3-4). In Scripture, "death" and "exile" are two ideas that belong together. The psalmist sees himself as rejected and cut off from God. He senses the weight of judgment (v 5-7). He is isolated from friends and feels restricted, as though he's in prison (v 8-9).

If dead, then he is without hope. God's miraculous acts are for those in the land of the living. Is he beyond reach now (v 10-12)? However, instead of giving up, he chooses to cry out to God in prayer (v 13-14). The song seems to finish abruptly without final deliverance or trust as he describes again the suffering he experiences. It seems that he has been left alone with only darkness for company (v 15-18).

···· **TIME OUT** ··

Many people have particularly identified with the words of this psalm when struggling with depression. Certainly, that sense of sinking into the depths, of imprisonment, isolation and darkness describe well the symptoms of depression. For those who struggle with low mood, there's great comfort here. However, this psalm is not purely or even primarily about mental illness. Rather, it points us to Christ.

Read Psalm 88 again, but this time imagine it is Jesus speaking the words.

⌄ Apply

Jesus is the one who was cast down to the depths, seemingly forsaken and cut off at the cross. It is because Jesus has gone down to the grave that hope is not extinguished with death. We have hope beyond the pit, beyond death, of resurrection life in Christ. This is good news for those tempted to give up whether because of suffering, depression, guilt or grief.

⌃ Pray

Do you know someone who appears to have hit rock bottom? Pray that resurrection hope will be reignited in them.

But don't leave them alone in the darkness. Verse 8 is a very real experience for people. So call or message to tell them that you are praying for them.

A son of disobedience

Hagar was foolish to despise Sarai, but she was sinned against as well as sinning. God's people don't always behave in a godly way, nor deal with the consequences well.

Read Genesis 16:7-16

Although God's mercy focuses on Abram, it is by no means confined to him. For the "angel of the LORD"—the messenger who speaks not only *for* God but *as* God—seeks out Hagar in her flight.

> ❷ *Why does God question Hagar (compare 3:9-10)?*
> ❷ *How does he address her?*
> ❷ *What other Bible events does God's promise to Hagar remind you of?*
> ❷ *What has Hagar learned about God?*

God questions Hagar to confront her with her situation. She is not the "wife of Abram" (16:3) as Muslim tradition has it, but the "servant of Sarai" (v 8) and if she had remembered this, things might have gone better for her. (The Bible, of course, sees nothing intrinsically wrong with one human being serving another in an unequal relationship, and nor should we.) Hagar is to abandon her plan, return to Sarai and submit to her (v 9).

✔ Apply

Notice how God hears and answers Hagar's cry even though she is rebelling and running away. God answers prayer by grace...

> ❷ *How are you tempted to think that God answers prayer because of how good, keen or spiritual you are?*

The surprise blessing

But Hagar is also given her own promise of blessing (v 10), which partially parallels that given to Abram (15:5). The child is named by God himself (in words that parallel those of the angel Gabriel to Mary some 2,000 years later), and his name, "God hears" (16:11), reflects God's attentiveness to Hagar.

Hagar's relationship with God has progressed. God has heard her, and she has "seen" him (hence the name she gives to God, v 13). Now she obeys him by returning home.

✔ Apply

Hagar's story has a "happy ending", but not one which the modern mind finds easily acceptable, as she once again becomes a slave.

> ❷ *What might this teach us?*

✖ Pray

Look back over the events of chapters 4 – 16 to remind yourself of the things you have learned about God's character and the way he deals with his people.

Thank him that we can trust him to be the same, and deal with us in the same way, today.

Be blameless

Thirteen years separate Ishmael's birth and Isaac's. But when God eventually appears again to Abram, his words call for careful reflection and understanding.

....

A conditional promise?
Read Genesis 17:1-2

- ❓ *What must it have been like for Abram and Sarai to have spent 17 years relying on a promise?*
- ❓ *What two things does God instruct Abram to do?*
- ❓ *Does this mean God will only keep his promises if Abram first obeys him?*

Initially, these verses seem to make the covenant promise conditional on Abram's own righteousness—if Abram is "blameless", God will confirm his covenant with him (v 1-2). Yet surely the promise is by grace ("I will", 12:2-3) through faith (15:6)? Yes, but… the covenant leads to a personal relationship between God and Abram, and it is that which comes into clearer focus at this point.

In 17:1 Abram is told (literally) to walk before the face of God Almighty—as Enoch did (5:24). This suggests Abram needs to be active—as with riding a bike, godliness is not achieved by standing still. Abram is also to be "blameless" before God. Because there is more to God than mere "might", there must be more to his servants than only passive obedience before a powerful deity.

Yet the covenant still rests on grace. For instance, there's no suggestion here that Abram's righteousness either demands or deserves reward.

There would be something deeply inappropriate about God blessing people as they dishonour and disobey him, and as they act with violence and injustice to others. Grace might produce such a situation, but neither grace nor faith could tolerate it. The covenant is *not* conditional. Yet, having created the opportunity for us to come back into relationship with our holy God, it demands that we are righteous.

.... TIME OUT ....

Read Luke 7:36-50

- ❓ *How does the woman illustrate the relationship between God's grace and our behaviour?*

⌃ Pray

Today, aim to do the good works God has prepared for you to walk in (Ephesians 2:10).

Pray that you will never take God's grace for granted.

The sign of circumcision

God's opening words to Abram in chapter 17 have introduced a fresh emphasis on the need for personal righteousness. But what is God's part in this "deal"?

Grace upon grace
Read Genesis 17:3-8

❷ *How many times does God say, "I will"?*

❷ *What's the main impression from these verses—a deserved reward or undeserved grace?*

Between verses 4 and 8 there is no hint of conditionality to the covenant. Instead, blessing is piled upon blessing. Abram has been promised a huge number of descendants (13:16; 15:5). But now God promises that from Abram will come not just *a* nation and a kingdom, but *nations* and *kings*. ("Nations" in Hebrew = *goyim*, which customarily refers to the Gentiles.)

So a name change is required (17:5). Abram, "Mighty Father", becomes Abraham, "Father of a multitude". And the covenant referred to in 17:7 should also be seen as extending to these "*goyim* and kings", though this lies in the future. The promise of the land is reaffirmed (v 8), but its blessings aren't only for those who live there.

The sign
Read Genesis 17:9-14

❷ *What did God tell Abram to do, and why?*

❷ *What would disobedience mean?*

Circumcision was to be the sign of inclusion in God's covenant, so Jews viewed circumcision and the covenant as virtually synonymous. But Paul points out the gap between the original promise and the sign of circumcision (Romans 4:9-11).

So why the delay? Surely because of what was about to happen. The conception of Isaac—the child of promise, who was to be born the following year—was imminent. But now, at the core of this act of conception (and every other conception until the Messiah came), there would be a token of bloodshed—the means of atonement (see Hebrews 9:22b).

✓ Apply

❷ *What has happened to the sign of circumcision since the coming of Christ?*

See Romans 2:29; Colossians 2:11-13.

⌃ Pray

Thank God for making you a member of his covenant people through the death of Christ.

A hilarious promise

"Abram" has become "Abraham", and God has told him that he will be the father of nations and kings. But how will that happen to the ancient couple?

Bitter laughter
Read Genesis 17:15-18

As with Abraham, God changes Sarai's name (from "princess" to "my princess") and highlights how she will be the mother of "nations" and "kings", underlining what he has already told Abraham (v 5-6).

- ❓ *Why, do you think?*
- ❓ *Why does Abraham laugh (v 17)?*
- ❓ *How have Abraham's expectations diminished?*

Notice that Abraham's response to God's message is not all it might be (v 17)! His laughter expresses bitterness, not joy. His plea on Ishmael's behalf perhaps reflects the diminishing expectation and growing frustration of the last 13 years (v 18). Wouldn't it be more straightforward to adapt to the present reality, rather than keep holding out for this "promise"?

⌄ Apply

- ❓ *Ask yourself if your own prayers aren't similarly "toned down" from what they once were, by the frustrations of experience.*

Joyful laughter
Read Genesis 17:19-27

- ❓ *How does God raise Abraham's expectations and reassure him about Ishmael?*
- ❓ *If Isaac is to be the son of the covenant, why does Abraham circumcise Ishmael?*

God will give Abraham real cause for laughter, with a son from Sarah (Isaac = "he laughs"). Ishmael will not be neglected (v 20, compare 16:10), but the covenant will pass to Isaac, who will be born in a year's time (17:21).

With this, God leaves Abraham, who sets about circumcising his household. The covenant sign is given to Ishmael and every male in Abraham's household—even those foreigners bought with money (v 23, 27). Though the covenant will pass to Isaac and his descendants (v 19), it nevertheless encompasses anyone and everyone linked to Abraham, which here already includes Gentiles.

⌃ Pray

Pray for gospel work among Jewish people, that many of Abraham's family may come to belong to his faith.

Strange visitors

There's a sense of mystery about the opening of this chapter, which clearly takes place not long after the previous story

Sarah is not yet pregnant with the child she will have in Abraham's 100th year.

Read Genesis 18:1-15

❓ *Who comes to visit Abraham and Sarah?*

❓ *What evidence is there that Abraham suspects the visitors' identity?*

❓ *The identity of the visitors makes this whole scene remarkable. In what way?*

The visitors are not seen as they approach, only when they have arrived (v 2). And although Abraham's greeting, and the provision of a meal, are customary of Middle Eastern hospitality (v 2b-8), we catch a sense of urgency in his instructions to Sarah.

Verse 10 confirms what Abraham evidently suspected—this is the Lord. And how extraordinary it is that God receives the hospitality of his creature! But there's a further purpose to this visit. Abraham is asked where Sarah is—for, even though the visitors' words are not addressed directly to her, they are certainly for her ears. And the message from one of them is that it's only a year before Sarah has a son.

Dangerous laughter

Re-read Genesis 18:11-15

❓ *Why does Sarah first laugh and then lie?*

❓ *What's the key sentence in these verses?*

Now it's Sarah's turn to laugh in disbelief (compare 17:17). But when the Lord repeats what both she and he have just said, fear compounds the problem—Sarah denies laughing. So there is a stern, if restrained, rebuke in the final words of the visitor.

✔ Apply

"Is anything too hard for the LORD?" (18:14). The answer is clearly "No".

❓ *What, then, limits what God will and won't do (See Romans 8:28-29)?*

⌃ Pray

And what about us? Perhaps you've prayed for years for a relative who seems so hardened to the gospel, or for a spiky and difficult work colleague. Do we secretly laugh at the idea that they could change? Do we give up praying? "Is anything too hard for the LORD?"

Read Ephesians 3:20-21. Repent of your lack of faith, and trust our supremely able God.

And then renew the prayers you have abandoned.

The God of justice

The Lord has delivered his message for Sarah, but now he is about to deepen Abraham's understanding of the covenant relationship…

Doing what is right and just

Read Genesis 18:16-21

❷ *Where is the Lord going and why?*
❷ *What is the reason why he decides not to hide his purpose from Abraham?*
❷ *What is the specific appropriate response that God expects Abraham to show, in response to God's grace towards him?*

The Lord is on his way to Sodom, to see if the accusations against Sodom and Gomorrah are true (v 20-21). Notice that God is not just a power to be called on, but the perfect, moral Judge of all mankind.

God will not hide what he is about to do precisely because of his covenant with Abraham—because Abraham is to be blessed himself and is to be the source of world blessing (v 18). We see again (17:1-2) that God's blessings call for an appropriate response from Abraham. He must not just passively receive what is promised, but instead become an active partner in the covenant. In particular, he is to instruct his children and his household so that they, like him (see 17:1), may also "keep the way of the LORD". And this is achieved by nothing other than "doing what is right and just" (18:19).

Understanding what is right and just

So God's way is to be Abraham's way and the way of those associated with him. Surely this is why God doesn't hide his forthcoming judgment from Abraham. If Abraham is to instruct others in God's way, he must understand that way.

Abraham already knows that God is the Almighty. It's no surprise that God could destroy Sodom. But Abraham needs to know that God is also righteous and just, so that he may teach others to do righteousness and justice, and bring blessing to the whole world.

☑ Apply

❷ *How convinced are you about God's righteousness and justice?*

Take time to think how you can teach others to "keep the way of the LORD".

All creation sings

If you were to write a song of praise about God, where would you start?

Read Psalm 89:1-18

❓ *What does the psalmist praise God for?*
❓ *Who or what else praises God?*
❓ *What is the source of rejoicing?*

Ethan the Ezrahite begins by praising God's character, specifically his love and faithfulness. God's love is eternal; it lasts for ever. God's love is seen in his covenant which he established with David and his descendants (v 1-4). It is important to begin here because it means that when Ethan goes on to praise God's sovereignty as demonstrated in creation, we can see that his providence is intended to serve the purpose of the covenant faithfulness of his love.

Creation declares the glory of God. This includes both heaven and earth, seen and unseen. The angels and glorious beings of heaven are creatures too. God is uniquely sovereign and uncreated (v 5-8). Angels, then, are not to be feared or worshipped, but their duty is to glorify God and point our worship to him (Revelation 19:9-10).

God reigns over the sea and the land. It is often assumed that ancient Israelites were fearful of the sea, seeing it as a place of chaos and danger, but the psalmist knew that God was sovereign there too. He could calm the waves and subdue sea monsters such as the mythical Rahab (Psalm 89: 9-13). This may also allude to the defeat of hostile empires such as Egypt. Rahab appears to have been a nickname for Israel's former oppressors.

The purpose of God's sovereign rule over heaven and earth, land and sea, is so that he might display his righteousness. His just rule is an act of loving kindness. Blessing and happiness belong to those who trust in the sovereign, righteous, loving and faithful God. They find joy and protection in him (v 14-18).

✔ Apply

Look around you and take in the beauty and glory of God's creation. Pause to think about all the different ways in which God has taken care of you through your life. All of these things are examples of his providence and intended to point to his love for his people in Jesus.

✔ Pray

Praise God for his character, especially his love. Thank him for the many ways you have experienced his love, care and protection.

Read the psalm again as your own personal expression of praise and trust in the Lord.

The Judge of all mankind

Abraham has a great commission—to teach others to be righteous and just, like God himself. But are God's standards of righteousness and justice compatible with ours?

Does God do what we recognise as right, or—as Muslims believe—is "right" defined as "what God does"?

Questioning judgment

Read Genesis 18:22-33

❓ *What is Abraham's concern with regard to God's forthcoming judgment of Sodom (v 23-24)?*

❓ *What's his concern with regard to God's character (v 25)?*

Abraham clearly knows that God intends to destroy Sodom and Gomorrah. And he must also know that Lot is living there. But he is concerned not only for Lot, but for the principle of justice: "Will you sweep away the righteous with the wicked?" (v 23).

But more than that, Abraham is concerned for the moral integrity of God himself. Twice in verse 25 he repeats: "Far be it from you" that God should act unrighteously. For if he does, then the whole universe is chaotic and amoral.

❓ *What conclusion do you think Abraham comes to by the end of his encounter with God?*

There is no standard of justice above God, and yet God is not "above" justice. Rather, perfect righteousness and justice are expressions of his very character. He does only what is right and just, and what is right and just is seen in what he does.

Bidding war

❓ *What do you think lies behind the "bidding war" that goes on in this curious conversation with God?*

❓ *What is at stake in God's answers to Abraham?*

❓ *What is at stake in Abraham's questions to God?*

The "bidding down" process reveals that the whole of wicked Sodom will be spared, if necessary, to save even a handful of righteous people. This reassures Abraham that God's justice is not arbitrary. The Judge does indeed act justly, and our human notions of justice do correspond to something in the character of God himself. When Abraham teaches people to do righteousness and justice, he can confidently direct them to be like God, not merely to obey him.

🔼 Pray

We too have been given a great commission (see Matthew 28:18-20). Pray for Christians struggling with doubts about God's justice.

And pray for God's righteous justice to fall on unrepentant cultures that oppose him— yes, even on yours!

Lot's danger

The trio who visited Abraham has split up. While the Lord himself stayed behind, the angels have gone on to Sodom.

Hospitality

Read Genesis 19:1-11

- ❓ *What would you say is Lot's motive throughout this story?*
- ❓ *What is the writer at pains to emphasise in verse 4?*
- ❓ *Some people suggest that Sodom's sin was their violation of hospitality towards strangers. But what do these verses tell us?*

The Middle Eastern obligation to provide hospitality falls automatically on Lot. Following custom, no offer is immediately accepted, nor any refusal allowed until the visitors agree to stay (v 2-3). But then the true character of Sodom is revealed—as every single man of the city (see v 4) turns out with the intention of raping the visitors.

What was Sodom's problem?

Clearly, it's ludicrous to suggest that Sodom's problem was simply a lack of hospitality! But this is not the "proof text" against homosexuality that some try to make it. Other passages (e.g. Ezekiel 16:49-50) suggest that it was not for sexual sin alone that God judged Sodom. The argument about homosexuality must be decided on wider biblical grounds.

Lot's behaviour in offering his daughters horrifies us, but don't assume that what the Bible describes, it approves. We've all seen news film of crowd violence towards unfortunate individuals. Lot faces just such a mob. He has an obligation to protect his guests. Should his guests be sacrificed? Or his family?

- ❓ *But is it really a case of "either/or"?*
- ❓ *What would you have done?*

Whatever the rights and wrongs of Lot's action, the mob refuses his offer and the angels intervene—the rescue of Lot is about to begin.

⌃ Pray

Lot's foolish choice of where to live has led him to this horrific situation (see 13:10). There is a straightforward lesson here!

Pray for those who, whether by their own fault or not, end up in such situations and must make "messy" decisions affecting the lives and safety of others.

Lot's rescue

It's now time for Lot to leave Sodom. Look out for the details in this story that emphasise God's incredible mercy.

Tough mercy
Read Genesis 19:12-29

- ❓ *Who is included in the offer of salvation?*
- ❓ *How does Lot respond to the angels' warning?*
- ❓ *How does God respond to this?*
- ❓ *How does God accommodate Lot's physical weakness?*
- ❓ *How is God's fairness—the issue that so concerned Abraham in 18:22-32—demonstrated here?*
- ❓ *Why is Lot saved (19:29)?*

Salvation is offered to those in Lot's family (compare v 12 with Joshua 2:18; 1 Corinthians 7:14). Unfortunately, the sons-in-law ignore the threat of judgment and are left behind.

But even Lot is lethargic about leaving! It seems incredible that after the previous night he still lingers (Genesis 19:16), but stress and panic can induce such strange behaviour and so the angels physically drag Lot, his wife and daughters out of the city. This act of riding roughshod over Lot and forcing him out is actually the Lord's mercy (v 16).

When Lot cannot find the energy to escape, he pleads to be allowed refuge in Zoar—and thereby saves it from destruction (v 18-21)! And so, as Abraham hoped, unworthy Zoar is saved because of the few righteous people now found there.

The destruction of Sodom, Gomorrah and the surrounding territory is swift and absolute (v 23-25). Lot's wife is destroyed when she cannot resist a last look (v 26). This seems harsh, but she disobeyed an explicit warning not to do this (v 17). Ultimately, there must be consequences to our disobedience.

In verse 29 we're told that God rescued Lot because he "remembered" Abraham, just as a similar "remembering" will prompt a deliverance in years to come (Exodus 2:24).

⌄ Apply

Don't "look back" in your Christian life. **Read Luke 17:32-33** and be warned.

⌃ Pray

God the Judge stands at the gate. Pray for a sense of urgency about your own salvation and the salvation of others.

ESTHER: When God seems absent

The big picture

Esther is known for being the only Bible book which doesn't mention God. But when his promise of a Messiah comes under threat, we see how God has been powerfully at work all along...

The story is full of startling coincidences and reversals, and reads almost like a pantomime: the beautiful rags-to-riches queen, the self-important, easily manipulated king, and the dastardly villain. Today we're going to zoom out and get a handle on the big picture, so that when we zoom back in again tomorrow, the details point us more clearly to God's big plan.

If you have time, **read the whole of Esther.** (It should take about half an hour.)

The Bible Project also has an excellent summary video here: bibleproject.com/explore/video/esther/. The QR code below will take you to the video.

The bigger picture

- **?** *Who are the four main characters?*
- **?** *What seemingly "random" events move the plot forwards?*
- **?** *What reversals do you notice?*

The whole book hinges on chapter 6, where, simply because the king can't sleep, the Jews are plucked from certain death and brought into abundant life. It's like God has stuck big red arrows all over the text, showing us his loving care for his people.

✔ Apply

Where are you experiencing God's absence at the moment? It could be personally, or in a relationship, or in a situation you're praying for, or something that's happening in the world.

- **?** *How does the big picture of Esther help?*
- **?** *How does the bigger picture of God's providential work in the world help?*

⌃ Pray

Pray that through our time in Esther, God would encourage you in the situation you've just thought about, helping you to notice his gracious hand at work and assuring you of his loving care.

Empty glory

Today, we're introduced to our first main character, supposedly the most powerful man in the world, King Xerxes (Ahasuerus in Hebrew).

Read Esther 1:1-2

The year is 480 BC, and although some of God's people have returned home from exile, many, like Esther, are still scattered throughout the Persian Empire. This was a vast geographical area stretching from Romania to Pakistan, and Libya to Kazakhstan, and also included the land of Israel. For the original readers, this was the whole world.

Look at me!

Read Esther 1:3-9

❷ *What clues are we given as to the impressiveness of the celebrations in each verse?*

For six months, all the important people of the empire are dazzled by Xerxes' glory. Then comes a week-long, whole-citadel party in outrageously lavish surroundings, with unlimited alcohol available to all.

❷ *How do you think the guests felt about:*
  • *the party?*
  • *Xerxes?*

This was the social event of the decade, a chance to feel part of the "in" crowd, to live the high life. It's the best the "world" has to offer. But it comes with a catch. What isn't clear to us, but would have been known by the original readers, was that Xerxes was making plans to invade Greece.

❷ *So why do you think he holds this elaborate feast (think about who he invited, v 3!)?*

In spite of the support he had gathered from all over his empire, Xerxes' invasion of Greece (which takes place between chapters 1 and 2) was a complete failure, and that is how he is most remembered by history.

❷ *How is the author being ironic in the impression he gives us of Xerxes?*

He may be king of the world, but he's just as weak as everyone else, and his glory is empty.

⌄ Apply

❷ *As you look around the world, what impresses you? What "in" crowd do you wish you were a part of? It could be looking a certain way, having a particular lifestyle or job, or gaining a respected position in society or church...*
❷ *How is this glory ultimately empty?*
❷ *What's the "catch" (see John 12:25)?*
❷ *How is what Jesus offers you better?*

⌃ Pray

Pray for wisdom to discern where you are being tempted away from Jesus towards impressive worldly things. Give thanks that the ultimate emptiness of worldly glory causes us to yearn for something better.

The folly of kings

Yesterday's passage described Xerxes' superficial splendour, glory and majesty. Today we see his true colours.

The king's shame

The party is in full swing, and the sloshed sovereign calls for his prized possession...

Read Esther 1:10-12

- ❓ Why does Xerxes command Vashti to be brought in?
- ❓ Why might she refuse?
- ❓ How does Xerxes react and why is Vashti's refusal such a problem for him?

It's not surprising that Vashti had no desire to be ogled by a load of drunk men. But talk about embarrassing moments! Xerxes looks like a total joke. How will he rescue his reputation?

The king's counsellors

There were no marriage counsellors in ancient Persia! Instead of being quietly resolved, the situation escalates...

Read Esther 1:13-22

- ❓ Where does Xerxes turn to for help with his wife troubles (v 13-15)?
- ❓ What does this tell us about the way he functions as a king?
- ❓ What consequences does Memucan foresee (v 16-18)?

We're already getting hints as to why the rest of the story develops as it does. A lot of it has to do with the way the insecure king is so easily manipulated.

- ❓ What are the consequences for Vashti (v 19)?
- ❓ Why do you think Memucan's idea goes down so well with the king (v 21)?
- ❓ But now the whole Persian Empire knows about the king's insubordinate wife! How does this make Xerxes look?

It just makes you cringe, doesn't it? Memucan is motivated by fear—he's got to tell the king what he wants to hear. An empire-wide decree denouncing Vashti and the proposal of a new, better queen are balm to Xerxes' humiliated soul. But ultimately, he still looks weak, because his advisors aren't able to tell him the hard truths.

⌄ Apply

- ❓ When you need advice, what is your first port of call?
- ❓ Do you also have wise people around you who will point you to your loving, all-wise, heavenly Father?
- ❓ When you are given advice, do you tend to listen to the bits that make you feel good and ignore the bits that don't? What will this lead to?
- ❓ What have we learnt about King Xerxes in chapter 1?
- ❓ How is Jesus a better King in every way?

⌃ Pray

Spend some time praising Jesus for being our perfect, sovereign, servant King.

The promised son

From seeing God's work in creation, Psalm 89 now takes a messianic turn as it thinks about God's promises to David and his descendants.

Read Psalm 89:19-37

❓ *Who is the figure that the psalmist now brings to our attention?*

❓ *How does God display his love and faithfulness through his covenant with David?*

The song now turns its focus onto David and his descendants. If praise for God is about his loving, faithful character and that character is most visible in his covenant, then the focus of the covenant is specifically on the line of David. David is chosen as a champion or saviour; he is the warrior who will protect and deliver God's people because God will strengthen him (v 19-21). In fact, God will fight for David and defeat his enemies (v 22-23). This covenant relationship is about love. It's about the Father's love for his son. Note that this means the son does the work of the Father. If God is sovereign over creation, then David too will have authority over land and sea (v 24-26). David is appointed "firstborn". Here this is about pre-eminence rather than chronology. David is pre-eminent as ruler among all other humans (v 27). God promises to establish David's kingdom for ever (v 28-29).

David's descendants might not live up to the same standards. In fact, to a man, they pretty much all fell seriously short. God warned that when they failed and fell, he would punish and discipline (v 30-32). However, God is eternally love and he is faithful to his promises. He will keep his covenant

with David; the kingdom will be established for ever (v 33-37).

···· **TIME OUT** ··

If you were a Jew living 2,000 years ago under Roman rule, you might wonder how God was going to keep this promise. The answer is of course found in Jesus. Jesus is the beloved son, firstly as the second Person of the Trinity, eternally begotten, and secondly reflecting his human nature as David's heir. He is the one that God the Father chooses to love, who does the Father's work and who is our strong Saviour, delivering us from the enemy of sin.

❓ *How does Jesus fulfil the hopes of this psalm in a way that David and his descendents spectacularly failed to do?*

✔ Apply

By seeing how this psalm applies to and through Christ, we can see in the gospel all the evidence we need of God's love and faithfulness. We can trust God to keep all his promises because he has kept his promise to establish his kingdom through Jesus and to save us at the cross.

⌃ Pray

Identify three precious promises from Scripture. Thank God for them and ask him to help you to trust him to keep them today.

Miss Persia Competition

Eventually, Xerxes comes to his senses and realises that he has no queen! Meanwhile, a young Jewish girl is quietly going about her business…

Cold comfort
Read Esther 2:1-4

> ❓ *Flick forwards to 2:16 and compare it with 1:3. Approximately how many years did it take for the king to calm down after the Vashti incident (2:1)?*
> ❓ *Remember that during this time, Xerxes had been away fighting his disastrous war with Greece. How do you think he was feeling by the time he came home?*

According to the ancient Greek historian Herodotus, Xerxes spent the rest of his life humiliated and wallowing in "sensual overindulgence".

> ❓ *What evidence for this do we see (v 2-4)?*

☑ Apply

Xerxes has failed as a warrior, and so he turns to home comforts to boost his ego.

> ❓ *Where do you turn for comfort when you've had a bad day? TV? Alcohol? Grumbling at anyone who'll listen?*

⌃ Pray

Give thanks for the comfort and hope that Jesus brings to your life. Pray that he would be more real to you than the physical comforts of this world, and ask for help to remember this the next time you're tempted to place your hope elsewhere.

Enter Esther
Read Esther 2:5-7

One of the big questions the book of Esther addresses is whether God's promises still apply to the Jews who have not taken up the opportunity to return from exile.

> ❓ *What do we learn about Mordecai?*
> ❓ *Why do you think the writer goes into so much detail about his background?*

Mordecai and Esther are from the same family as King Saul (see 1 Samuel 9:1). This will become significant later…

> ❓ *What do we learn about Esther?*
> ❓ *What would it have been like for her, growing up as an orphan from an ethnic minority?*

Notice the way the writer is building up the story—could you guess what happens next?

⌃ Pray

At this point, Esther and Mordecai have absolutely no idea what's going to happen—they can't see the end of the story. But when they looked back later, they'd be able to see how God had been putting all the pieces of his plan in place right from the beginning.

Whatever you're going through at the moment, pray for faith to trust that God is at work, putting his pieces in place, achieving something very good.

Choosing God's way?

Today's passage is a moral muddle of questionable choices. But they're the same kind of choices we face every day.

....

Read Esther 2:8-11

Esther doesn't seem to have had a choice about entering this beauty contest—she's trafficked to the palace along with many other young women.

- *But what decisions does she make (v 9, 10)?*
- *Look carefully at the middle of verse 9. Which Jewish laws would Esther presumably have had to break? (See Leviticus 11 if you're stuck.)*
- *Why do you think Mordecai forbids Esther from revealing her nationality? How do you think he's feeling in Esther 2:11?*
- *What do you make of their motives here?*

We can't ultimately know what was going on in Mordecai's or Esther's minds, but the undercurrent is one of fear. In that climate, they needed to cooperate and keep their heads down if they wanted to survive. They may be morally compromised, but their weakness and mistakes can't throw God's plan off course.

And the winner is…

Read Esther 2:12-18

- *How does Esther give herself the best chance possible of becoming queen (v 15)?*
- *What would happen to her if she didn't succeed (v 14)?*

- *How is God at work here?*

Failure was a pretty bleak prospect—Esther would become a disused concubine, shut up in the harem for the rest of her life, with no freedom, no family, and very little status. But success involved throwing the Jewish law out the window and then doing her utmost to please a pagan king she wasn't yet married to.

✔ Apply

- *Think of an area of life where you face a choice between God's way, and the world's way. What are the consequences of each?*
- *Think of a situation where you're struggling to discern what God's way might be. What are your heart motives?*
- *Do those around you know that you're a Christian? And do they know what it means?*
- *When are you tempted to compromise in order to fit in and avoid trouble?*
- *How have you seen God graciously use your bad choices for good?*

⌃ Pray

Pray through your answers to the apply questions, confessing your sin and asking for courage to change and wisdom to make God-honouring choices. Give thanks that God is bigger than our bad choices.

The plot thickens

Today we're introduced to the central antagonist of the book, who is contrasted in every way with the protagonist, Mordecai.

Merciful Mordecai
Read Esther 2:19-23

Mordecai now appears to be some kind of court official, possibly as a result of his connection to Esther. He has every reason to hate Xerxes for essentially abducting his cousin, yet he is fulfilling Jeremiah 29:7—"seek the peace and prosperity of the city to which I have carried you into exile".

> ❷ *How is Mordecai rewarded?*
> ❷ *What effect do you think this incident might have had on Xerxes?*

✅ Apply

It would have been easy for the Jews to resent their Persian rulers. But Mordecai obeys God, even though it does him little good. Why not look out for opportunities to enact "secret" kindnesses today, for God's eyes only?

This little incident is quickly forgotten. We'll have to wait until chapter 6 to find out what God was up to. How does this help you to be patient as you wait for God to reveal his purposes in the puzzling things of life?

Hateful Haman
Read Esther 3:1-6

> ❷ *Given what we've just read in chapter 2, what's the surprise in 3:1?*

As we saw in 2:5, Mordecai was from King Saul's family. Haman is descended from Agag, king of the Amalekites. Saul and Agag were mortal enemies (1 Samuel 15).

Mordecai refuses to bow down not because he resents Haman for getting the top job, but because Haman is an enemy of God's people—an enemy of God.

> ❷ *How does Haman feel about Mordecai's "disrespect" (Esther 3:5)? What does this tell us about his view of himself?*
> ❷ *Why do you think Haman decides to involve the entire Jewish race (v 6)?*

Like Goliath in his scaly armour (see 1 Samuel 17:5), Haman is a child of the serpent, whose defiance of God and his people will ultimately lead to his downfall.

✅ Apply

We may not be maniacs waiting for an excuse to commit genocide, but seeds of Haman's sinful attitude can be found in our hearts too.

> ❷ *Do you ever overreact when your pride is dented? How?*
> ❷ *What's the Christlike alternative?*

🔼 Pray

Give thanks for Jesus, who didn't stand on his rights, but humbled himself to the lowest place for our sakes (Philippians 2:5-8).

Disaster strikes

Bad news for the Jews: the guy who wants to wipe them out also happens to have the king of the world in his back pocket…

The plan is agreed
Read Esther 3:7-11

- ❓ *How much time has passed since Esther became queen (compare v 7 with 2:16)?*
- ❓ *How does Haman try to persuade the king to go along with his plan (3:8-9)?*
- ❓ *What reasons does Haman give for why the Jews should be killed (v 8)?*
- ❓ *What questions might you expect Xerxes to ask at this point?*
- ❓ *But given what we know of Xerxes' insecurity and weakness, are you surprised at his response (v 10-11)?*

✔ Apply

It seems outrageous—how could Xerxes go along with it when he has no evidence at all that Haman's claims are true? But aren't we just the same, trusting people who butter us up? How can we make sure we're acting with integrity (see Psalm 119:105)?

The date is set
Read Esther 3:12-15

- ❓ *What is at stake here in terms of God's promises (remember that the Persian Empire included Israel and all the exiles who had returned)?*

The edict goes out in the first month of the year (v 12), but the date set for the annihilation isn't until the twelfth month (v 7).

- ❓ *How do we see God's hand in controlling the "lot" (= dice)?*

It's no wonder the people are left "bewildered" (v 15). This is truly horrific. But the timescale, rather than delaying the inevitable, allows God's salvation plan to unfold over the following 11 months.

---- **TIME OUT** ----
Read Psalm 2

- ❓ *How does this give you a glimpse into the wider picture of what's going on in Esther 3?*

^ Pray

Great news for the Jews: Haman's power is no more than a flea shaking its fist compared to the power of God. But so often, we feel utterly bewildered in the face of suffering, oppression or opposition.

Spend some time praying for yourself and for others around the world, that God would help us to see things from his perspective.

Pray that instead of despairing, we would continue to put our hope in the one who holds the lot.

If I perish…

The king's edict goes out on the eve of the Jewish Passover festival. Just as everyone was getting ready to celebrate, joy turned to devastation.

Sackcloth and ashes

Read Esther 4:1-5

- ❓ *How do Mordecai and the Jews respond to the news (v 1-3)?*
- ❓ *Why do they do this?*
- ❓ *What isn't mentioned, but we can assume they were doing it too?*
- ❓ *What do we learn about Esther in v 4-5?*

It seems that Esther alone of the Jews doesn't know what's going on yet! We're left wondering how she will react…

☑ Apply

Just as God isn't mentioned, neither is prayer. But fasting, sackcloth and ashes are "code" for prayer—even the pagan Ninevites prayed in Jonah 3.

- ❓ *Under what circumstances do you pray the most? And the least?*
- ❓ *Does your prayer life reveal a deep dependence on God? What might need to change?*

Deliverance arises

After five years of marriage, the king doesn't seem to be quite so keen on Esther. Will she be able to help?

Read Esther 4:6-17

- ❓ *What is Hathak's role in the narrative?*
- ❓ *What is Mordecai's plan (v 8)?*
- ❓ *Why is Esther reluctant to go to the king (v 11)?*
- ❓ *How does Mordecai persuade her (v 13-14)?*
- ❓ *How do both Mordecai and Esther show that they're trusting God here?*

Hathak's head must have been spinning! But in all the to-and-fro, Mordecai's message hits home: he sees God's hand in placing Esther in this position close to the king, and (quite forcefully!) encourages her to step out in faith. Back in chapter 2, Esther did what was morally ambiguous to preserve her life, but now, she's willing to risk her life for what's right, and throws herself on God's mercy in prayer.

- ❓ *How is Esther a little shadow of Jesus here?*

God's people need a mediator to save them from death, one who is prepared to die for them.

☑ Pray

Esther was resigned to death, but had hope that she might succeed and survive. Jesus knew death was the only way to save us, and yet chose it willingly.

Give thanks for Jesus, your mediator, who gave his life to save yours. Pray that the truth of Jesus' extraordinary victory over death would fill you with brave faith to live God's way in a hostile world.

Bad to worse

Today's passage is a bit like the set-up episode before the big-money action takes place, as God moves all his pieces into place…

Dinner for three

It's an incredibly tense moment: will the king be in a genial mood today?

Read Esther 5:1-8

> ❓ How do you think Esther is feeling as the scene progresses?
> ❓ How has God answered the prayers of Esther and the Jews?
> ❓ Why doesn't Esther just get straight to the point? Why the elaborate banquets?

What a relief it is in verse 2 when Xerxes holds out the sceptre! It seems uncharacteristically gracious! But Esther then holds her nerve, proceeding with the plan God has put in her mind through those days of praying. She has to be very careful. After all, the king is implicated in Haman's plot—he gave it the ok! The more she can please him, the better. And tomorrow, we'll see God's hand powerfully at work in delaying her request until the second banquet.

⌄ Apply

The Jews are by no means out of the woods, but it's a promising beginning. Are you good at remembering to thank God for the little answers to prayer as well as the big?

Pride comes before…

The camera now pans over to Haman, who has no idea what's in store for him.

Read Esther 5:9-14

Haman sounds like a conceited child in the playground as he recounts his successes to his nearest and dearest.

> ❓ Where does Haman get his happiness from (v 9, 11-12, 14)?
> ❓ What threatens his happiness (v 9, 13)?
> ❓ How is Haman really just as easily manipulated as Xerxes?
> ❓ Unless something changes, where will Mordecai be by the time Esther gives her second banquet?

⌄ Apply

Haman is glory-hungry, desperate to fill his inner emptiness with the praise of others.

> ❓ How do you see similar tendencies in yourself?
> ❓ How do you feel when people don't appreciate you? What will this lead to?
> ❓ How does knowing that your identity is rooted in God's love for you in Christ, not in the opinions of others, lead you to true happiness and freedom?

⌃ Pray

Ask for a deeper understanding of what it means to be accepted by God, and pray that this would free you from enslavement to the approval of others.

Heavy lies the head

In Psalm 89 we've seen that God's character is defined by loving faithfulness and the evidence of this is that he has kept his promise to King David. But there is a twist in the tail.

As we come to the end of Psalm 89 we see God's faithfulness questioned.

Read Psalm 89:38-52

❓ *What has happened to the king and the kingdom?*

❓ *What does this seem to say about God's love and faithfulness?*

❓ *What does the song plead for?*

The twist comes as the psalm describes a scene of desolation and destruction. God has rejected his "anointed one", the king and heir to David. The psalmist claims that God has gone so far as to renounce his covenant, to go back on his word. The crown is "defiled" (v 38-39).

Without Yahweh defending the king and the kingdom, it has quickly fallen to enemy powers who mock and scorn. The stronghold of Jerusalem is in ruins. Enemies rejoice. It is as though God has not only failed to show up for Israel, he has actively opposed her (v 40-45).

This leads to a plea so frequently heard in the pages of Scripture: *How long O Lord?* The psalmist pleads for God to return to his former love, to not give up on the king. He reminds Yahweh that the mockery is against HIS "anointed one" and so against God himself (v 46-51). Yet the psalm ends in an expression of trust and praise; clearly Ethan has not given up all hope (v 52).

···· **TIME OUT** ·······································

It seemed as if the covenant was being revoked as the people went into exile in Babylon. All the promises had failed. No king, no city, and temple worship at an end.

However, God's greater purpose was to raise up his ultimate anointed one, a King who would reign on David's throne for ever.

⌄ Apply

God's loving faithfulness is doubly seen in Christ. He is David's heir, the eternally loved Son. He is also the one who God, in his great love, sends to take our place so that we know his love and forgiveness.

Jesus was also the anointed one who experienced rejection and defilement. He was scorned and mocked. He was considered cursed, though not for his own sin: "He was pierced for our transgressions" (Isaiah 53:5). This should encourage us to prioritise bringing the good news of God's loving faithfulness to friends and family.

⌃ Pray

Choose three friends to pray for who don't yet know Jesus. Pray for opportunities to introduce them to the faithful, loving God.

The humble lifted up

Here, in a chapter dripping with irony, we have the first of many remarkable "reversals" in the book.

What a coincidence!

Read Esther 6:1-3

- ❓ *How many "coincidences" can you count?*
- ❓ *How is God at work in these events?*
- ❓ *How do these verses explain what God was up to back in 2:21-23?*

What if Esther had only given one feast? What if the king hadn't suffered a bout of insomnia? What if a different book had been chosen? What if a different page had been read? What if Mordecai had been honoured at the time, five years before?

✔ Apply

- ❓ *How has God used insignificant events to alter the course of your life and bring you to where you are now?*
- ❓ *How does this encourage you today?*

Honour given

Read Esther 6:4-14

- ❓ *How is Haman feeling as he waits to see the king (remember 5:14)?*
- ❓ *How does this feeling increase by the end of 6:9?*

Imagine Haman's face in verse 10. It must have left Haman reeling in shock. Instead of gleefully murdering Mordecai in a public spectacle, he's forced to parade him through the streets as the most honoured man in the land.

- ❓ *How is he feeling by verse 12? And how do his wife and friends interpret the situation (v 13)?*
- ❓ *How has Mordecai's situation reversed from that of 4:1?*

It's beautifully satisfying, isn't it? We're left almost feeling sorry for Haman, such is his downfall. But there's much worse to come, as this enemy of God's people comes up against the one true God.

✔ Apply

- ❓ *Can you think of a time when God graciously humbled you to protect you from ruinous pride?*

James 4:6 says, "God opposes the proud but shows favour to the humble". It can be hard to accept this in a world where self-promotion seems to work. How will today's passage help you to trust this verse?

✔ Pray

Give thanks that every aspect of your life is under the control of our gracious God.

And give thanks that in God's kingdom, the first will be last and the last first (Luke 13:30).

The truth at last!

Chapter 6 ended on a very foreboding note for Haman. He has no idea yet, but his bad day is about to get immeasurably worse.

Esther makes her move

Read Esther 7:1-4

- ❓ *How does Esther again use her God-given wisdom in trying to get the king on-side?*
- ❓ *What risk is she taking by revealing her Jewish heritage?*
- ❓ *How has she grown into her role of mediator for her people?*

Back in 2:10, Mordecai instructed Esther to keep her heritage quiet, probably because it was safer for her. But now Haman's threat has arrived, she risks everything by approaching the king (5:1-2). Now, here she is putting her life on the line again, identifying herself with the condemned Jews because it's the only way to save them.

⌄ Apply

- ❓ *What difficult things might God be asking of you?*
- ❓ *How can you step forward in faith?*

Justice done

At last, the villain gets his comeuppance, and it's brutally ironic.

Read Esther 7:5-10

- ❓ *Compare 5:11-12 with 7:5-6. How have things changed for Haman now?*

In one day, he's gone from boasting that he's the royal couple's best friend, to being utterly terrified before them. And it's all because his sin has been exposed.

- ❓ *What two things make Haman's terrible guilt look even worse in the king's eyes (v 8, 9)?*
- ❓ *What is so fitting about Haman's ultimate fate (v 10)?*
- ❓ *Proverbs 5:22 says, "The evil deeds of the wicked ensnare them; the cords of their sins hold them fast". How have we seen this to be true here?*

⌄ Apply

- ❓ *In what ways are you discouraged by the success of the wicked, both on a personal and a global level?*

Haman's fate is a shadow of what will happen to all wickedness on the day when God rights all wrongs. How does this help you to persevere in living God's way? How does it cause you to pray for those who are living in rebellion against God?

⌃ Pray

"God made him who had no sin to be sin for us, so that in him we might become the righteousness of God" (2 Corinthians 5:21). Give thanks that although we too deserve the terrible fate of the wicked, Jesus has endured it on our behalf so that we can have eternal life instead.

Not out of the woods yet…

Haman may be gone, but his sinister legacy lives on.

Read Esther 8:1-6

❓ *How do verses 1-2 complete the reversal of Haman's and Mordecai's positions?*

❓ *What does Esther's emotional state reveal about her heart?*

❓ *How has Esther's faith been transformed through the twists and turns of what has happened?*

❓ *How does she see herself now (v 6)?*

Yesterday we saw how Esther had grown into her role as she trusted God. But today's passage goes even further, as we're given a glimpse right into the core of what makes her tick. Where before she was isolated from God's people, living a pagan lifestyle and hiding her faith, now she publicly identifies herself with them: these are her people, her family, and she loves them. She will do whatever it takes to save them, boldly approaching the king because she now recognises how God has put her in this position "for such a time as this" (4:14).

⌄ Apply

How has God used unwanted challenges to change your spiritual trajectory for good? Maybe a job you didn't get, or a relationship that didn't work out? How has he protected and preserved your faith by closing the "wrong" doors?

⌃ Pray

Ask God to help you to keep trusting his loving sovereignty, especially when it feels like God is closing the "right" door.

Oh Xerxes…

Read Esther 8:7-8

❓ *What do you make of Xerxes' response here? How does it tally with his previous behaviour?*

❓ *How might he be feeling about his own part in Haman's plot (see 3:10-11, 14)?*

How embarrassing! He's accidentally sentenced his queen and her people to death, and now Xerxes can't even think of a way to sort it out! There's certainly no apology, just a complete denial of responsibility. Yet again, he demonstrates his weakness and total inability to rule wisely.

❓ *What's the big problem with saving the Jewish people (8:8)?*

❓ *How is God at work for good here?*

Xerxes could have refused to allow any kind of rescue plan because he would look so idiotic—after all, it was his name and ring which had sealed the deal (3:12). But just as Xerxes had gone along with Haman's evil plan, he now agrees to rubber-stamp whatever Esther and Mordecai can come up with. Tune in tomorrow to find out what it is!

An ingenious solution

When you spill red wine on the carpet, you can't undo it, but you can cancel it out by spilling white wine and salt over the top (supposedly).

Counter-decree

Read Esther 8:9-14

- ❷ *What is Mordecai's answer to the problem of the irrevocable law?*
- ❷ *How do verses 11-14 parallel 3:13-15?*

What's new here is the mention of the Jews' "enemies" (8:11, 13). It seems it wasn't just Haman who was anti-Semitic. There were some in the Persian Empire who were delighted at the prospect of legally annihilating the Jews. What difference will this second decree make?

- ❷ *How long will the Jews have to prepare themselves for the attack (v 9, v 12)?*
- ❷ *How does this show God's grace in the casting of the "pur" back in 3:7?*

Nine months is enough for the message to get through to the whole vast empire, with plenty of time left for preparations.

☑ Apply

The king can't revoke his decree—he needs to issue a counter-decree instead. The cross works in a similar way. The wage that our sin deserves is death. But God issues a counter-decree to save us from this penalty (Romans 6:23). Sin is still paid for—not by our death, but the death of his dear Son.

Spend some time thinking about Jesus' astonishing sacrifice for you, and give praise to God.

Reversals galore!

Reversals are in all the best stories—Cinderella, Joseph, Star Wars, Pride and Prejudice...

Read Esther 8:15-17

- ❷ *How is 8:15 the reversal of 4:1?*
- ❷ *How is 8:16 the reversal of 4:3?*
- ❷ *Why do people actually become Jews?*
- ❷ *How is this another reversal?*
- ❷ *The Jews haven't actually been saved yet. Why are they so happy?*

☑ Apply

The story of redemption is the greatest reversal ever. We were dead in our sins, now we're alive in Christ. We were God's enemies, now we're his friends. We were condemned, now we're justified.

- ❷ *What other gospel reversals can you think of?*

We haven't reached the new creation yet. We're still deep in the battle against sin, sorrow and the devil. But should we not be even happier than these Jews in Persia?

⌃ Pray

Give thanks that Jesus' death and resurrection guarantee our future hope. Pray that the joy of this truth would fill you today.

Just judgment falls

The fateful day has finally arrived. Many in the empire have sided with the Jews, but there are still plenty who want to kill them.

God's victory
Read Esther 9:1-10

❷ *Why do you think the Jews have so many enemies (There was an element of truth to what Haman told the king in 3:8)?*
❷ *How difficult is it for the Jews to gain the upper hand?*
❷ *How do you see God at work in this?*
❷ *Why do you think the Jews don't lay hands on the plunder, even though the decree said they could (9:10)?*

(Hint: Have a look back at the error King Saul made during his defeat of Haman's ancestor Agag in 1 Samuel 15:2-3, 7-11.)

The Jews recognised this as a holy war, just like Saul's war with the Amalekites. God was using them to root out his enemies—it was for him, not for their own personal gain.

❷ *How does this passage bring home to you the seriousness of rebellion against God?*

More bloodshed?

Brace yourself, it's not a comfortable read! But it's in God's word for a reason.

Read Esther 9:11-19

❷ *Why does Esther ask for another day of fighting in Susa?*

We feel distinctly uncomfortable about all this killing, and wonder how God could approve. But we need to remember that the Jews aren't just lashing out unprovoked—these people are trying to kill them. And God is just. This means that he must punish sin and evil. In the Old Testament, he uses his chosen people to bring about this justice.

☑ Apply

❷ *How does the cross change the way we are to respond to the sin of others (Romans 12:17-19 might help)?*

Jesus has paid for the sins of Christians, so we are to forgive them. And those who are not Christians will pay for their own sin —so we are to forgive them too (and warn them). Either way, it's not up to us to make retribution—it's up to God.

❷ *How does this challenge you?*

⌃ Pray

Ask that you would be able to forgive those who sin against you because God has forgiven your much greater sins against him.

Promise-keeper

In our final day in Esther, it's time to zoom back out and look at the big picture once again.

Read Esther 9:20-28

- ❓ *Why do Jewish people celebrate Purim? How do they celebrate it?*
- ❓ *Why is it called Purim? How is this a reminder that God was in control all along?*
- ❓ *The Persian Empire was so vast that it included Judah, Jerusalem, and virtually all Jewish people. What would have happened to God's salvation plan if Haman's plan had succeeded?*

If there were no Jews, there would have been no Jesus. That's how important the events of Esther are.

King and queen?

The Jewish monarchy was over by this point, but God provides leadership for his people in another way.

Read Esther 9:29 – 10:3

Remember Queen Vashti? She seemed to be little more than an ornament, queen in name, but not in role. What about Esther?

- ❓ *How does she function as a true queen?*
- ❓ *How does Mordecai fulfil the role of King of the Jews?*
- ❓ *How is he a shadow of Jesus here (10:3)?*

Mordecai, dressed in royal purple robes and a golden crown (8:15), seeks the welfare of God's people.

The big question asked by the book of Esther is whether God will stay faithful to his promises even though his people have been unfaithful to him—they're dispersed throughout the Persian Empire, with no Davidic king, and no longer following the sacrificial system.

- ❓ *What's the answer?*

⌄ Apply

The story of Esther has shown us that even when he seems absent, God is in fact powerfully at work behind the scenes, keeping his promises. He saved his people from annihilation and, a few hundred years later, sent the promised Messiah. At the darkest moment of history, when Jesus was dying on the cross, God seemed absent. But behind the scenes, he was achieving our spectacular salvation. And now, as wars rage and rulers scoff at God, he might seem absent. But he is still powerfully at work, keeping his promise that one day, our true King will return, bringing with him perfect justice, joy and glory for his people.

- ❓ *How does the story of Esther help you to yearn for Jesus' return?*

⌃ Pray

Ask God to take the truths you have learnt from studying Esther and bury them deep in your heart, so that you are changed from the inside out.

Introduce a friend to

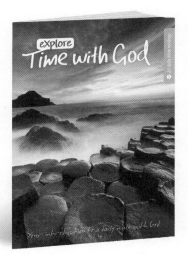

explore

If you're enjoying using *Explore*, why not introduce a friend? *Time with God* is our introduction to daily Bible reading and is a great way to get started with a regular time with God. It includes 28 daily readings along with articles, advice and practical tips on how to apply what the passage teaches.

Why not order a copy for someone you would like to encourage?

Coming up next…

- ● Genesis 20 – 50 *with Tim Thornborough*
- ● 2 Timothy *with Phillip Jensen*

- ● Christmas: The sweet, sweet names of Jesus *with Tim Chester*

 Don't miss your copy. Contact your local Christian bookshop or church agent, or visit:

UK & Europe: thegoodbook.co.uk
info@thegoodbook.co.uk
Tel: (+44) 0333 123 0880

North America: thegoodbook.com
info@thegoodbook.com
Tel: 866 244 2165

Australia & New Zealand:
thegoodbook.com.au
info@thegoodbook.com.au
Tel: (+61) 02 9564 3555

South Africa: www.christianbooks.co.za
orders@christianbooks.co.za
Tel: 021 674 6931/2